4PM Town Hall

**DISCOVER YOUR SKILLS,
LEVERAGE THEM AND FIND YOUR DESTINY.
A STARTUP ADVENTURE.**

Bishal Kumar

(BHU, NITK SURATHKAL, 10+ YEARS WITH MNCs, FOUNDER)

INDIA • SINGAPORE • MALAYSIA

Notion Press

No.8, 3rd Cross Street
CIT Colony, Mylapore
Chennai, Tamil Nadu – 600004

First Published by Notion Press 2021
Copyright © Bishal Kumar 2021
All Rights Reserved.

ISBN 978-1-63781-477-2

This book has been published with all efforts taken to make the material error-free after the consent of the author. However, the author and the publisher do not assume and hereby disclaim any liability to any party for any loss, damage, or disruption caused by errors or omissions, whether such errors or omissions result from negligence, accident, or any other cause.

While every effort has been made to avoid any mistake or omission, this publication is being sold on the condition and understanding that neither the author nor the publishers or printers would be liable in any manner to any person by reason of any mistake or omission in this publication or for any action taken or omitted to be taken or advice rendered or accepted on the basis of this work. For any defect in printing or binding the publishers will be liable only to replace the defective copy by another copy of this work then available.

Praise for 4PM Townhall

"Bishal Kumar weaves a gripping story of resilience, grit, agility, and execution in his book - '4pm townhall'. Plenty of food for thought for leaders, entrepreneurs and people want to make things happen."

~Simerjeet Singh - International motivational speaker, leadership coach

"Bishal is a very enterprising person, always focused on finding solutions to any challenges - personal or professional. He has consolidated his experiences and knowledge in this book and it's worth reading !!"

~Manoranjan Kumar - Author, The Art of Getting Things Done

"Must read book for entrepreneurs, how to take your startup to success"

~Vishal Thakur - NITK, Vice President in Goldman Sachs

"An inside story of indian startup ecosystem with challenges and takeaways that is going to help many startups to save their life and others to grow next level, Go for it. A great story with awesome values."

~Vijetha Shastry - TiE Bangalore(Director), Ex-NASSCOM, Ex-Taj

"Getting into a startup is one thing and taking it to success is another. In 4PM Townhall, Bishal uses compelling real-world situation solutions and templates that will startup and leaders."

~Sumit Prakash - NITK, IIM, Consulting Manager at Cognizant

"Book offers an overwhelming journey through implementations, pain, love and Success. 4PM Townhall examines how an individual facilitates various problems into quick solutions in his journey. Good Work Bishal!"

~Rajat Jain - Amazon bestselling Author, Floating Happiness

"You can always correlate some of the characters present in the book to someone you would have bumped at some walk of life. In Bishal's book, I could find myself close to Farida…" [Part taken from the Foreward]

~Nidhi Raj, BHU (Gold Medalist), IIT Roorkee (Gold Medalist), Data Scientist, Massachusetts, USA

"Getting into entrepreneurship is a bold step. You need to have a clear view about what you are going to build. The big picture. But it is also very important to understand the ground reality. This books Bishal takes us to a journey of an entrepreneur at the ground level and shares the experiences of kind of issues, a young entrepreneur is likely to encounter."

~Mihir Kumar - IIT Kharagpur, Texas A&M, Data Scientist

"Loved the read. Apart of engaging fiction, contains wisdom to create success story despite love and loss."

~Ankesh Kumar - CS, LLB, Ex-CS HPCL-Mittal, Co-owner Citi Mega Mart

Praise for 4PM Townhall

"4PM Townhall book is very well done. The minute I started reading it, I knew it was exactly what I was looking for. I spent a few hours reading and learning from your books and was impressed to say the least."

~Vivek Barnwal - QA, Accenture

"Book offers an overwhelming journey through implementations, pain, love and Success. 4PM Townhall examines how an individual facilitates various problems into quick solutions in his journey."

~SK Gupta - CEO, Coders brain technology

"Entrepreneurship is dreamt by many but the thought of failure often hinders the decision to take the first step. For people already begun with a start up, the hickups take a toll. This book is filled with real life experiences, stories and learnings which are of immense help to budding entrepreneurs and start ups. It offers an overwhelming journey through the thick n thin of life and resonating these to business. 4PM Townhall is a great work by Bishal providing real world situation solutions and templates for start ups and leaders. Enjoyed reading this."

~Varsha Gaikwad - Wealth Advisor, Mitraz Financial

"The author Bishal takes us to an entirely different world of Startup Entrepreneurship with lots of practical points for anyone to succeed in real life challenging the obstacles by turning them to opportunities."

~Vijayadasa Udupa - B.E.(Mech),F.I.E, F.I.V

"This book is very well done. The minute I started reading it, I was very well relate to the flow of the content. Helped refreshed my old memories. This book is clear and concise and offers much more information than I expected. Thank you and I am looking forward to."

~Ravi Linganuri - AntHive Tech, CEO

"4PM Townhall is new book of author Mr. Bishal Kumar. I have seen his knowledge and had chance to work with him. This book will help to understand challenges in Startup and specifically for new entrepreneur. My best wishes."

~Gaurav Chauhan - CEO, StatsMetrika Services

"This book is full of knowledge and soft skills that a person can imbibe and utilize in there career to prosper. Startup decisions and lifting it to pinnacle is all we can learn from this book. This is must read book for those who uses excel in there day-to-day life."

~Ajit Kumar - Performance Specialist, Hewlett Packard

"It's a brilliant price of work that collects years of entrepreneurial learning and provides a framework to start a venture! A great read for first generation entrepreneurs."

~Shiv Kumar - Head of Business Analytics, Mahindra and Mahindra

"This book offers an overwhelming journey through implementation pain, love and success. 4PM Townhall took us though, how an individual facilitates various problems into quick solutions in his journey at startup."

~N Madhusudan - Food Supply Chain Lead, Future Retail

Praise for 4PM Townhall | 5

"Never-Give-Up attitude is the first and foremost requirement which drives any entrepreneur and especially so, during the thick and thin of his/her professional journey and Bishal has always demonstrated this quality for more than a decade now, during which, I have got a good opportunity to guide and mentor him. He follows the apt quote verbatimly... "If you think you can, You can. If you think you can't... well, You are Right."

-Rakesh Barnwal - Serial Entrepreneur, CEO, FinancialIQ

"Very good book, Awesome contents, Well decorated with easy to understand Images."

-Indra B Prasad - Technical Architect, Capgemini India

"So real and practical! Bishal's book 4PM Townhall is amazing as it talks of real situations and challenges in his entrepreneurial journey and how he tackled them. A must read for anyone set on the path of entrepreneurship or achieving something new."

-Bhagaban Behera - IIT Kharagpur, CEO, Walrus Labs

"Bishal's book is very well done. The minute I started reading it, I knew it was exactly what I was looking for. Even though I knew Bishal as a friend and his journey as an IT Professional and an entrepreneur, reading his book was not about going through memory lane. It did has very fresh perspectives and in very much sync with what most entrepreneurs need to begin with. Book is very articulately written and believe me going through it will enrich budding entrepreneur's business wisdom and will save them a lot of time."

-Dr. Abhay K. Tiwari - PhD, Computational Science(IISc Bangalore)

"This book is a complete package for all startup enthusiasts to understand the startup journey, challenges faced, how to accept failures, and take its learnings to the next big step. It is good to see more such amazing tips being mentioned in this book which is surely going to benefit people from different areas to build exciting tools."

-Kavya Ramaiah - Software Developer 3, Arvind Internet

"A must read book for young to be entrepreneurs. Bishal has written the book from his life's experience. This are many things which you can use to replicate and achieve your success."

-Satish Kumar - NITK, PGDBM(XLRI), Faculty Christ University, Jain, Symbiosis

"For me this book was like opening up some old golden days memories of my startup(RentalAgreement) journey with Bishal himself. This book is full of motivation and take you to the ride of entrepreneurship days (good, bad, worst, great). and shows how a salaried employee can turn himself into entrepreneur and gets whats he always dreamed for (Love abundance of wealth & a peaceful journey).

Couple of lines that touched me: 1: Rajeev to Jim => You join now as a co-founder or join later as an employee. 2: Jim (Thinking in himself) => A ship in harbor is safe, but that is not what ships are built for."

-Nakul Nagariya - Technical Consultant, Capgemini

"Great piece of work. Loved the simple and straight to heart story."

-Dr.Ashutosh Singh - Physiotherapist, Narayana Hrudalaya

"There has been always an extraordinary difficulties behind every successful leader. But taking an initiative is important. Hope it will be a symbol for upcoming leaders."

-Nityen Prakash - Founder, Builds Worth Digital Marketing

"Taking a startup-decision and living it to success is a dream-come-true journey for any entrepreneur. 4PM Townhall brings an exceptional work resonating to many common challenges & handy solutions."

-AMARESH JHA - Life Coach, Trainer, Director, A.J Academy Life

"Getting into a startup is one thing and taking it to success is another. In 4PM Townhall, Bishal uses compelling real-time situations and templates that will help startups and leaders."

-Amanpreet Singh - Blogger at Happy Realization

"I wouldn't be surprised if 4PM Townhall someday becomes the new go-to guide for new-age entrepreneurs."

-Amit Kumar - CEO, WebOrion™

"I am endorsing this book because I feel that it is an excellent book which reflects the journey and struggles of a common man to become an entrepreneur and also it is a mini guide for spreadsheet."

-Jitendra Narayan - Principal, Govt. Polytechnic College, Ranchi

"Book offers an overwhelming journey through implementations, pain, love and Success. 4PM Townhall examines how an individual facilitates various problems into quick solutions in his journey."

-Dayanandsoni - SMM, Lead generation Expert, youtuber

"I have known Bishal for a long time and have seen him grow in his career with sheer hardwork and keeping his feet on the ground. He has put really wonderful efforts in bringing this book together. It definitely resonates with his commitment and dedication to everything else in life that matters to him. I am happy to see Bishal achieve another milestone and become an author."

-Prateek Tandon -Business Analyst, Oracle, Wipro. Founder-Bizadspac

"4PM Townhall reveals the true Success Mantra for all the Entrepreneurs - 'Perseverance' and 'Hardwork'. The success toolkit mentioned in every chapter unfolds the profound experience of the author and it is certainly a must read book for every Entrepreneur."

-Mahidhara Davangere V - MBA, MFC, AIA(UK); Actuary & MD, Pramartha Group

"When somebody has seen multiple failures, they have tasted the opposite side of what glory for most of us means. It either is the worst of what one could have tasted or best of anything that could have ever happened to them. It's a matter of how they take it and what they make out of it. Bishal is one of those go-getters who evolved out of every tough phase, and took the leap to bring 4PM Townhall into reality. Don't miss the chance to immerse into this wonderful read filled with unlimited inspiration from the first word to the last dot.

-Sujit Lalwani - NITK, Serial Entrepreneur, CEO, iU e-Magazine

Contents

About the Author 9

Acknowledgment 11

Thanks Love 15

Foreword 17

||||| Part One |||||
Know Your Own Theory

The College Chapter 22

||||| Part Two |||||
Follow Intuition, the Truth

Corporate Life Begins 48

||||| Part Three |||||
The Seven Lessons to Not Fail in Startup

The Startup that Burns 76

||||| Part Four |||||
How to Setup a Winning Business

A New Beginning from Scratch 98

||||| Part Five |||||
The Framework to Success

Journey of Reaching His Destiny 134

Epilogue *163*

Images from Author's Diary *167*

Zero-to-Advance Package on Spreadsheet from Author *173*

Another Book from Author Desk *177*

About the Author

Bishal is a 1985-born, with academics from India's Esteemed Colleges – Banaras Hindu University, NITK Surathkal and IFIM B-School. He is a core executioner, who has turned multiple real-problems into running businesses. His debut book 'Your Leadership Playbook' presented concise powerful tips as a quick read on leadership practises and well-praised by readers. This book '4pm Townhall' is a full-stack (covering all stage) leadership journey with a gripping storytelling and take-aways. He is passionate about Process Initiatives, Technology, People Coordination, Structuring, and creating system with Google sheets.

Bishal lives in Bangalore with his wife Anamika and daughter Ahaana.

Apart worked with World's Best MNC for 10Yrs, Bishal is also known for

- Founder, RentalAgreement.in
- Co-founder, Bucketkart
- Organizer, startup forum 'Neighpreneur'
- Founder, Online Solution Matrix
- External Faculty – NHCE and Oxford College of Engineering
- Volunteer, Parikrma – NGO for Child Education
- Member, VFC Community & Art of Living
- Multi-tasker & Spreadsheet(Excel) Expert at various platforms

www.facebook.com/author.bishal
www.instagram.com/author.bishal

PRAISE FOR AUTHOR

"Relentless go-getter individual"

– **Rakesh Mishra, Serial Entrepreneur & Coach, StartupGamePlanning**

"Process person and has an eye to connect the dots"

– **Girija Prasad Swain, Startup Mentor, COO at WorldHaus**

"Never-Give-Up attitude"

– **Rakesh Barnwal, Serial Entrepreneur, CEO, FinancialIQ**

"An extremely hard-working with Mathematical abilities, a perfect problem solver"

– **Mahidhara Davangere V, MBA, MFC, AIA(UK); Actuary and Managing Director, Pramartha**

Acknowledgment

I am deeply grateful to so many people whose presence in my life added the right emotions, to being able to pull out a story, which I hope you will enjoy. My sentiment is aptly expressed by Albert Einstein, who said "Every day I remind myself that my inner and outer life are based on the labors of other men, living and dead, and that I must exert myself in order to give in the same measure as I have received and am still receiving."

The book helped me break out my intellectual isolation during Covid-19 pandemic. I dived into many interesting imaginations. Taking this opportunity to heartily thanks to my wife – Anamika. Without her support and intellectual inputs this book never would have happened, and in case happened would have been so jumbled-up. I am so lucky to have her as my partner in all ways of my life. Blessed to have a daughter, Ahaana, for putting me through the delighting moments.

I have been a constant dreamer in my life, and thanks to the stimulation of discussions with people who gave me space, who intrigued me, to be myself – Naina Narayan and Rakesh Mishra. I feel blessed and grateful to meet Amit Jha, Harshna Tharayani, Kunal Kant, Prabhat Ranjan (bokaro), Amit Ranjan, Sneha Agarwal for the support & unstoppable belief in me (sometimes even more than me). Milan (barnwal), you were one whom I used to seek-out for anything and so many things, be it love attempts at school or placements, missing those dude. Thanks from core-of-heart. Dear Richa (Sis-cum-friend), hours pass like seconds and even common activities with you become moments of life; I feel so humbled and blessed with your invaluable presence in my life.

A very special thanks to Nidhi Raj, Priya Rungta, Ranjeeta Jha, Pravanjan mishra, Archana Keshav & Saurabh Rahul for the care, support, contributions and intellectuals into writing.

And here-after Just not able to resist myself for so many names that will follow…

My heartfelt thanks to Anik, Vijay Yadav, Roshan, Vijay Mahali, Milan Barnwal, Sukesh Choudhary, Kunal Singh, Chandan Jha, Suprabh Prakash, Saurabh Mehndiratta, Mithilesh; Loving-seniors: Mohit Chopra, Sumit Prakash, Ashish Kumar, Manish Thakur, Aashish Upadhyay, Gaurav Jain, Chandan Kumar; Pavithra Shenoy, Swathi HR, Nanda, Ravi Mehrotra; Avinash Kumar (Accenture, USA), Rajat Jain, Manoranjan Kumar (Author), Ankesh Gupta; Mentors: Tim Springer, Amit Pandey, Girija Swain

Wholehearted thanks to all my mates & patrons without you guys, I won't be what I am today. Please do pardon me personally, if I missed any expected.

With deep gratitude, I acknowledge my second parents and well-wishers uncle Mr. Shree Narayan & aunt Smt Usha Devi for their profound influence on my life and thinking. It is a blessing to have such a supportive and loving family – my mother Kiran Devi, father Madhusudan Prasad, mother & father in-laws Vijay Lal & Asha Devi, Pankaj, Lalita, Niraj, Anita, Raj, Neha, Saurav, Ritu and to our half-dozen Lovely kids - Ayush, Akansha, Akshat, Ahaana, Ridhhi, Arpit.

I also acknowledge to all thought leaders, motivational speakers, without the knowledge learned from them, I could have not written any potential valuable words.

Most importantly, I acknowledge and thank God for the blessings and warmness I have felt throughout this project. You are the source of all principles and all activity, I am a mere channel.

Thanks Love

"Wife is a better-half to her husband", you must have heard. During the book writing, I experienced it. Literal. Tons & tons of thanks to Anamika for her immense contribution towards book completion; be it writing numerous contents, or modifying and making it more presentable. Her dedication and keen interest towards making every content appropriate was astounding.

Yes, many of the contents in the book that you find interesting, high chance that It has been exaggerated and beautified by Anamika. And, many stuffs you may find boring, high chance that It has been enforced by me.

She has been the first editor, critic, and all-around supporter throughout this journey despite of her engaged schedule while raising a notorious toddler. During this 4pm Townhall, I actually got to see her untapped potential to rightly put the thoughts and imaginations. I am truly blessed to have a partner like her.

I am thankful for her compassion at several instances like

> *Anamika: Did you see the maid downstairs today"*
> *Bishal: (with joy) "Yes, Even she wished me with Good Morning!"*
> *Anamika: "Was it yesterday or today?"*
> (...and She was right, it was yesterday)

And thanks for understanding me, sometimes more than me. :)

To my caring and beautiful wife Anamika Saurabh, Sr Quality Analyst, 8+ Years Exp.

Foreword

I still remember my first Chemistry Practical class at BHU, Varanasi (India). I was anxious about who would be my lab partner. A tall thin guy with glasses, curls and a confident smile who had the same feature as the protagonist of the book, Jim, appeared. We introduced ourselves and soon the Chemistry practical classes were fun-filled. Our college book is full of stories – the indelible ones which definitely I am going to pass on to my next generation and Bishal would be one of the leads. We graduated from the same department with flying colors and beautiful memories. We took different paths but would always consult each other when stuck on the career path. However, the flow of inspiration was always from his side, with Bishal sharing new ideas and ventures whenever we talked.

Bishal has a dynamic personality and a lively character. He is always in quest of doing something different and impactful on all fronts and this book manifests innumerable glimpses of the same. With multiple startups incubated by him, and taken to a profound stage without solid backup is commendable and inspiring.

The book presents the journey to a successful venture. It highlights how petty challenges which we face in our day-to-day life can become the platform for opportunities and innovation. Through Jim's adventurous journey, it describes how one needs to break the ice of a comfortable salaried job and live to your dreams with endurance and perseverance. The later section mentions the different pillars of starts-ups and how all of them need to come together to build a solid foundation. The visuals in the books are intuitive and self-explanatory.

It will be a ready-to-go guide for entrepreneurs & leaders from various dimensions. This is going to keep you awakened to create your goals, and act as a catalyst towards success. If you are looking for a mentor to save your business from burning, then you are holding the right book. The grievous lessons from startup is demonstrated well, so yours should be safeguarded. It also brings, how you can create amazing tools & systems that can minimize the Time & Cost at every level.

> *In this story, he(Jim) broke down, he lost his well-paid job, time and money but didn't sit quietly after losing a battle; rather he came back stronger, and was able to make his way to several milestones. And so you can!*

The Dias of the book is set on a contemporary platform which keeps you engaged while injecting small doses of skill. You can always correlate some of the characters present in the book to someone you would have bumped at some walk of life. In Bishal's book, I could find myself close to Farida.

I extend my best wishes to Bishal and hope the audience enjoys and derives insights from the book to build a successful career path. Good luck for 4pm Townhall!

Nidhi Raj
Banaras Hindu University (Gold Medalist),
IIT Roorkee (Gold Medalist),
Lead Data Scientist - Pristine Infotech,
Massachusetts, USA
09 January 2021

PART ONE

KNOW YOUR OWN THEORY

The College Chapter

Are you an Introvert, whose majority of thoughts resonate to the internal world; or an Extrovert whose thoughts are loud, exciting and free-spirited? These are two types of human psychology which we are a part of.

And further, each of us prefers one of these cognitive functions – (i) Judging or (ii) Perceiving; and naturally rely on it in everyday situations.

(Credit: Jung, Founder to analytical psychology, early 20th Century)

Yin-Yang: Two halves that together complete wholeness. Symbolised as complementary (rather than opposing) forces that interact to form a dynamic system in which the whole is greater than the assembled parts.

"Bruce lee" (Film and martial arts legend known for his lightning quick fighting style) added two arrows around the Yin Yang to represent the continuous interplay of the two parts and a Chinese phrase that says: "*Using no way as way, Having no limitation as limitation.*"

A decade ago… At a world-class university, Uttar Pradesh, India…

The pleasant breeze with bright sunshine was spelling energy and making the morning blissful; it was almost 9:30 in the morning, the hostel-lobby was lively marked by adult males of all varieties, half-clad to well-dressed gentlemen; decked up to their best capacity to attend the Maths lecture by Prof. Bindra, the head of department (H.O.D. – Mathematics).

"Please bring form B1, with supporting documents to the college", the SMS popped-up on my Nokia phone (Nokia, at that time, had a market share of 51%, largest vendor in most countries). I was left at the center of a crossword puzzle, "what the hell is this form B1". "Krishna" – I yelled, "did you receive any SMS bro?", but Krishna shrugged his shoulder as if he just came from the ancient age, and took another yawning with eyes half-open. Krishna Yadav was the best missing link of the nocturnal species in the hostel, he just came out of his bed, while others were running to the canteen for breakfast.

That lethargic gesture from Krishna left me with no option, but to juggle from within the congested lobby, and in a matter of a few seconds, I was knocking on room number-71, which broke the morning catastrophe with the blockbuster song "Dil chahta hai…" (from an awesome movie starring Amir Khan). In a flash of second, the door opened and a tall figure with grim face, flexed cheekbones, broad smile hugged me and pulled me in.

Room number-71 was the eminent source of all the giggles, laughters, debates, and event plans for our small gang, it was Dev's room. I couldn't hold myself, and threw the same question, but Dev with wide-opened eyes stood dumbstruck, enacting **surprised** emoji.

"Then is he our last hope?" I uttered and he nodded his head like Rajesh Khanna*.

Jim Kaushal was almost 5 feet 11 inches tall, athletic build-up, sharp nose, dark eyes, with a bold & confident look; a look that is enough to grab your attention. He was like a double edged sword, handsome appearance, and flawless execution. He was a different species in the entire lot. There was a perfect blend of schedule, proactiveness, social life, sports and academic activity, and generosity in his personality.

We were heading to Jim's den, the treasure room of solutions to all our problems. As we reached, we saw a big lock on his door. Understood, he had already reached the canteen for breakfast. We headed promptly, and caught him up, there. "Jimmy!" I shouted, he turned his head, lifted his plate and invited us to join him with a persistent smile.

I was so engulfed with the curiosity of form B1, that I couldn't contain myself and just burbled out my question. He kinked his lips to one side in his charismatic style, slurped the all-time favorite soupy-maggi, and said "Breathe man, have some". I and Dev were assured now that Jim Kaushal had accomplished the feat once again. The canteen staff "Ram dayal", who used to serve the tea often said with an added innocent smile that, 'Jim bhaiya (elder brother) is the smartest & adorable guy in the whole campus, since he joined the college.'

---

* Rajesh Khanna is an Indian actor, film producer and politician, also referred to as the "First Superstar" of Indian cinema.

Know what delights you & others

His (Jim a.k.a. Jimmy) life wasn't like that of a common man who wants the world to go with his words and appreciate him. Rather he dedicates himself to win every situation by winning hearts. In our life, no one will remember how you **Looked, Walked or Talked** or what you did… Everyone just remembers you, by the way you **Made Them Feel** when they were with you.

Jim continued to delight people around him *NOT by doing different things, but by doing the things differently;* and of course, the secret of winning the hearts continued for 3 years.

Jim was a soft-hearted guy, with a genuine smile on his face. A random talk with him was enough to hypnotize you. With this reverent amalgamation of qualities, he carried a high esteem that was not just favourite among the boys, but was a darling of the girls as well.

"Life is a Race and every small thing does matter in it", he mentioned always.

Unlike most of the students, he used to wake up with guitar, at 5:30 sharp in the morning along with his artistic tabla[*] player roomy, preparing for his own best version. Usually, his day started with jogging in the hostel ground, followed by football practice, then going for routine classes. Once the classes got over around 4pm, he had his Spanish class for 45mins, and then a little bit of football again. Evening tea times were meant for fun with loving friends, and finally the day ended with guitar or dance practice for one or the

---

[*] tabla is an indian-origin instrument, consisting of a pair of drums

other events. **All these sound like a heroic scene from a movie, but trust me this was his real life that everyone in the college witnessed.**

Image: *A duet performance of tabla and guitar at inter-college fest. (Sketch by Author's artist cousin Abhishek Narayan).*

Jim loved running his fingers through guitar strings, wherein, his roomy stumbled the hostellers with musical beats over a pair of Tabla.

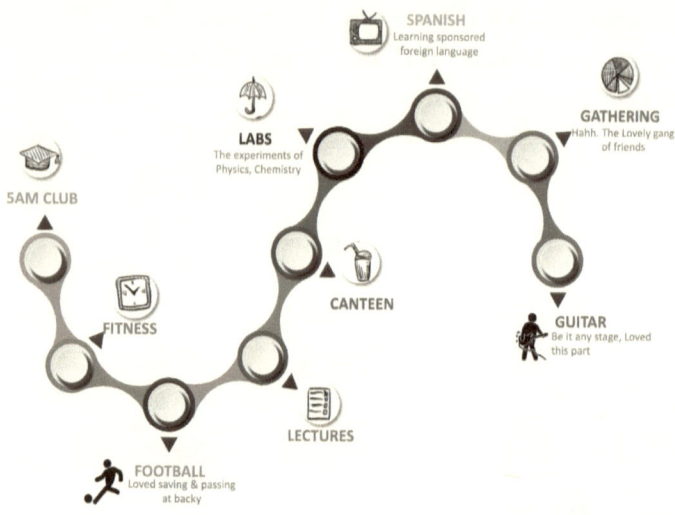

Image: *A usual routine from life of Jim*

From monitoring the class to leading an event, or from convincing the librarian to waive off the fine, to talking to canteen-wala bhaiya over the list of snacks; his magical words touched every heart in every corner. Jim could sense that his true potential lies in "***his ability to deal with people; his ability to arouse enthusiasm among people, he is working with.***" The years so far went happily, without much anxiety or stress; but only action.

Actions define you, not the knowledge

Jim took many initiatives during his college days for better management and systems, which made him a people magnet. He likes recalling a few:

1) 700+ people as one unit for a cause

It was a time when the Reservation Bill was introduced by the Government of India for Other Backward Class (OBCs). That was going to be enforced in our university as well; which sounded more of a political gimmick creating disparity between people. Well, the great part about considering the Bill was, many OBC candidates were going to be benefited nationwide, but would there be justice for other truly deserving candidates who were not falling in the reservation categories? The enactment of the OBC Bill would have also replaced righteous candidates with low-grade engineers, doctors & professionals in our society.

"Why can't they bring in the system to provide better infrastructure, enhance facilities, rather than voicing out for reservation," all these thoughts couldn't let him sleep for two nights.

The man who believed in action went on the ground with his four friends across each department and hostels, be it Nilgiri House or Shivalik House. He went on discussing with all the department representatives, and in absence of one, helped appointing one. Every single word and minute were valuable and taken on a conscious note; and at the same time, he valued other's time and opinion. During the course of action, he also got an opportunity to enter the Girls hostel, a completely different planetary experience.

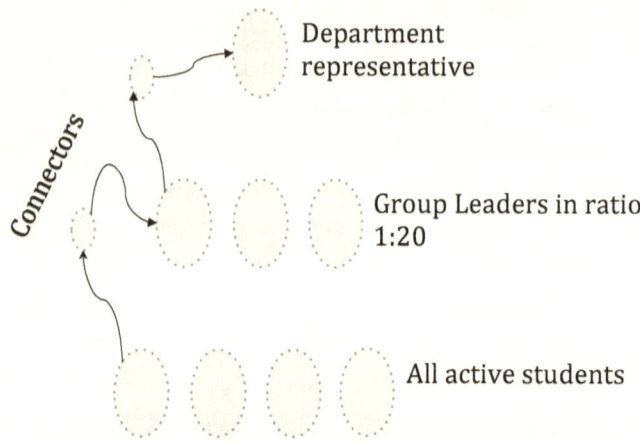

Image: *Three-level system towards preparing a big engaged community.*

Within a day, the system was ready with 3-Tier architecture at each department. Jim & his four friends communicated with all departments and legal authorities. The second layer consisted of the best supporters identified based on trust & energy level, and lastly, all the audience to whom Jim ensured the first group catchup as a single-family, and repeated the same in intervals. There were six coordinators/connectors who rigorously exchanged information between departments, ensuring complete focus on the predefined actions. Connectors were keeping the big family intact.

Image: Anti-reservation organized and peace protest

These moments were so enthusiastic that one just let-go off their food, their sleep and what not; and still would feel content; with the best leading example Jim himself. He would channelize his every thought & action. What an unprecedented outcome it was! The whole university was standing as one Unit, voicing for one Cause. The stature caught the attention of local authorities, governing bodies, and covered by all news channels. It was just an unforgettable experience for all: Jim, the university, students, and fellowmen.

2) Fish market into de-facto system in a Passport-fair

The community hall was fully crowded on the 1st day, as nearly 500 students gathered to apply for the passport. Being at IT college, the procedure to apply and receive a passport was shorter & easier, having college as a recognized address.

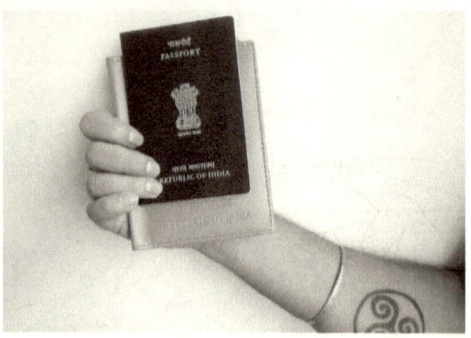

Image: *Passport*

But managing this activity was a nightmare. The passport registration process was set up in a hall which had two entrances (gates) The students entered from both the gates and soon the place was crowded with noisy students that were pushing each other to get them enrolled first. The management of this crowd was out of control for the security staff.

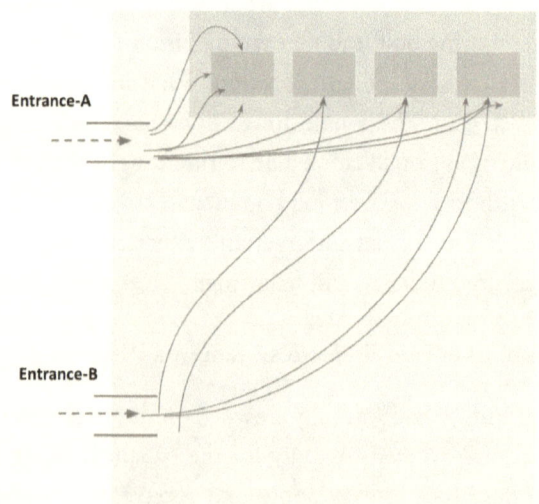

Image: *Appointment-hall (Before)*

Next to the entrance, 4 desks were placed with the government representatives taking the details of the students and processing it for further rounds. Being an unorganized structure, there was no transparency whose name is registered and who was left behind, the counter guys were shouting to call out their names and numbers. The whole place looked like a big Fishmarket with multiple sellers and a herd of customers. Jim was also one amongst the several students in the Fishmarket-cum-hall, exasperated by the whole approach. The unorganized approach led the activity to go out of control, on the very first day.

Jim, back to his room, quite frustrated… taking evening tea, sitting in the open area outside the canteen. For the next 20 minutes he kept thinking "We being in one of the Top IT colleges, are unable to drive such events in a smooth & peaceful manner, then imagine the situation in an unorganized sector or society where people are not much educated."

"Imran, Did you get your turn?".

Imran was crossing the passage of the lobby, turned towards Jim and nodded his tired face, "No Man. It didn't look like we would get our turn, so I left at 4:30 only", Imran replied with a sarcastic smile.

His inner thoughts were on fire and screaming within.

He realized once again *'Where there is a challenge, there is an opportunity',*

With a lion attitude, he called his room partner, few batchmates, discussed with them, and came up with a quick strategy to drive it.

Next day morning around 8 am, Jim reached 10 mins early. Before the students could enter from both the gates, he closed the back-gate himself. Now the whole crowd had to enter from one gate only. Jim, sitting near the gate, asked everyone to enter their details one by one in the register. The registration proceeded well without any noise or chaos. He was maintaining the register himself and coordinating with the representatives to take it further. As the crowd began to grow, candidates were informed about their time for appointment, so one can either wait in the hall or come back at a projected time (10min per candidate), based on a token number shared when registering with Jim. The whole activity went systematically & peacefully.

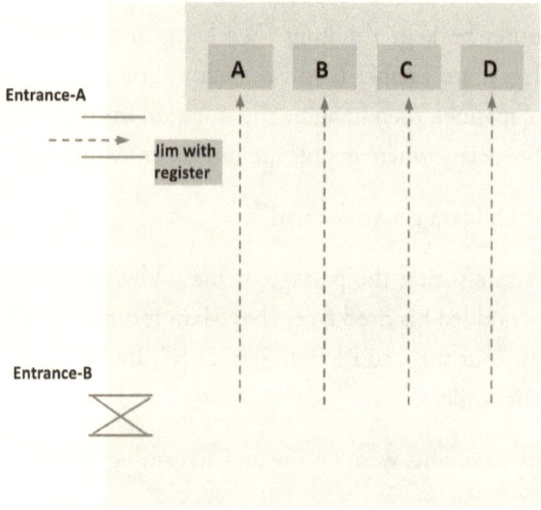

Image: *Appointment-hall (Jim's execution)*

What this Execution-specialist did, was not something miraculous but his *Accountability & Approach* drove the whole activity exceptionally.

Whether it is our college or workplace or a public place, people like blaming the system, instead of taking an initiative or coming out of their comfort zone. It is not always a big action that works, the willingness to act with positive intent and the next visible action is enough to play a magical role.

Meets the tattoo girl

Placement at college was taking its pace. When all friends were discussing companies, profiles, good role or high pay, life as a Civil Engineer, life as Software Engineer; Jim happened to meet a girl who was living in her own world with her own rules. "*Farida*" was a class topper and a sincere girl; punctual in class, No bunking despite any pressure from batchmates, the same outfit be it any occasion and a tattoo of a flying-horse on her forearm.

Image: *Farida with a flying-horse tattoo*

All these used to make her unique from the rest of the world, a persona that Jim had ever met in his life. She was so introverted, that she never said any extra words beyond the topic of discussion. All these persisted until now, however, things were going to change...

Upon their few catch-ups during Chemistry lab, Farida, for the first time in her life, felt like meeting someone who had quite similar thoughts (apart from her Ammi jaan – Mother), and a great sense of honesty & trust to people.

They both started meeting frequently either in the lab, canteen, or the library.

The girl who didn't spend a minute for a chit-chat with her batchmates in the class, was seen spending hours with a guy discussing career, life and many things. Surprising but interesting!

She started sharing her personal views with someone without hesitation, this had not happened ever before. She went on expressing many things like a free soul – about her close cousins, why she only trusted her mother, why she never liked people, how she skipped her uncle's bad intentions, why she had that horse tattoo, and many more.

She found a certain unique sense of freedom with Jim that transformed her altogether.

On the other hand, Jim too felt more of himself with her. He was going in flow with sharing his views and enjoying her company like never before. A month passed by sharing beautiful time, it came so far that Jim was sensing the perfect situation of taking this outside the college, for next life.

However, one thing was bothering him, hence, he started keeping a barrier. The Hindu-Muslim cultural lectures; that was plugged-in by his close uncle & hence-forth Jim's all family – "*Son, make anyone your friend, but not Muslims*". His mother used to tell him.

Then one day, his romantic dream life got toggled, up-side-down. He disconnected with Farida abruptly. Fullstop. No calls, no meetings. In true senses, It burnt his heart, left him almost dead, it was hard, very hard.

It was a short visit of Jim's mother to college; being the last semester she planned to visit for closing formalities. She got to know everything. Thanks, to those generous friends who knew everything, even more than Jim could even dream of. Knowing the matter, how could she (mother) say 'Yes' for a Muslim girl/community. Forget about planning a future, not even a friendship was allowed. She gave her swear and took a promise to discontinue this friendship.

Jim was disheartened. He didn't want to break anyone's heart like this, that too because of these illogical beliefs made & persistent in the society. On the other hand, he had to keep his mother's words too.

Such blind & bitter conformity by family and society kept bothering Jim for long.

...and so he made his mind that he will take a ***path of courage***, and **not opt for conformity** to this coward society – as large as 95% of lively creatures. He would ask the right questions to himself and others. He might get slow, he might not be a fast mover, but would *be the **Best mover with his***

own terms and conditions. He aspired to become a part of the 5% category.

* * * * *

Transformation in final year

It was almost the middle of 4th year, unlike the previous year, the classes were not full of lovely talks or routine things; it was the time to play strong & stay unbeaten as this year was destined to give the career, a kickstart.

"The twinkling stars in the sky looked like talking to me." It was 11 at night while sitting in the dead-end of the hostel lobby, inhaling fresh air. "I heard an inner sound like it wanted to say something", Jim was himself with me. He continued to rephrase those inner voices, "Jim, this is going to be the last year. You have to stay unbeaten this year too. Do you remember last year's election, cheers and the loud voices? Those were clear indications that they are indeed happy with the way you are leading everything and want you to do consistently." Those were so encouraging, Wasn't that?

Jim was now in constant turmoil and often talking to himself. The time was close for the Final Year Election too, where performers from different departments would file the nomination. If someone was recognized as the best performer for 3 consecutive years, then he/she would also be titled in "**Powerhouse Hall of Fame**", who represents the college in international consortium, a title that created history and was absolutely rare. The selected candidate would be recognized by the Ministry of Education, which in itself gave a unique identity and made the world see him/her differently.

Image: *Hall of Fame*

This was the time for Jim to work on his potential and achieve his next version of achievement. Days were passing rapidly, he was left with limited time to find a perfect balance between choices – his n-number of activities, or career, or both.

Formula to stay connected

It seems now Jim's name was gradually losing the charm in the talks, the positive vibes that used to create lightning were losing the intensity; apart from a few who were still delighted with his presence.

He was constantly annoyed and neck deep into sea of questions –

"Is there something missing from my end?"
"Is there a key to have a natural connection and enthusiasm alive?"
"Is there a secret sauce?"
(He kept thinking for some time... and finally...)
":-) YES", he answered himself with a smile.

"People feel aroused with true enthusiasm; **not** due to pressure or any materialistic favor, but because of praise... and being an honest listener to them."

Somehow he was not giving the same attention or importance to all of that he used to give before. He thought that, to shape up the career he must give studies a high priority, and at the same time charm of the delightment factor should not be lost, hence he was looking for some formula to stay connected with everyone with lesser efforts and time.

Be it wishing birthdays, any special day or planning for a surprise occasionally. All these touch people's emotions and let you connect with them.

Being the captain maintaining the data, events, and tracking them were a part of his responsibility. With great power comes great responsibility. And this tracking was troublesome if he didn't have any system in place. Aah! A pretty challenge – may be diary entry and scrolling for dates. There had to be some better way, something really fast and accurate.

"Where there is a challenge, there is an opportunity".

It was a long lunch break; while discussing these with fellows, his roommate (the Tabla player) mentioned about

"Prof A.K. Verma", a faculty from the Statistics department, "has got amazing tools that can manage huge data and tasks automatically".

Ohhh, what is it? Let's go and find it, Jim whispered to himself rushing to the Statistics department, just 100 meters, away from the canteen.

> *Verma sir is sipping tea in a white golden-lined cup with Good-day smiling cookies in his favorite red plate. Jim enters the room, touches his feet as greetings, and mentions his challenge. Requests to help him understand the tools that are being used by him. Verma sir, proudly turns his computer screen towards him and asks to sit closer. "This is called Google Sheets, one kind of spreadsheet, similar to Microsoft Excel, if, you have heard. It can do all kinds of calculations, reports and magics that you may have never thought".*

Verma sir also showed how he managed all the records of different batches, with names, exams, their scores, and dashboard to see the top scorers within one exam or across exams, Top scorer for the previous years, and whatnot.

Those emails & reminders that go automatically from his account, all of that... Just Wonderful!!

Mr. Verma explained the FIVE crucial elements of Spreadsheet:

1. **Spreadsheet** – Also called workbook. The tool itself.
2. **Sheet** – The different tabs within workbook
3. **Cell** – The smallest unit or piece that will hold the value, namely A1,B1,A2...

4. **Row** – Horizontal set. A cell is identified with "row number" as one part, say, 1,2,3...

5. **Column** – Vertical set. Gives the first part of the Cell's address, say A,B,C...

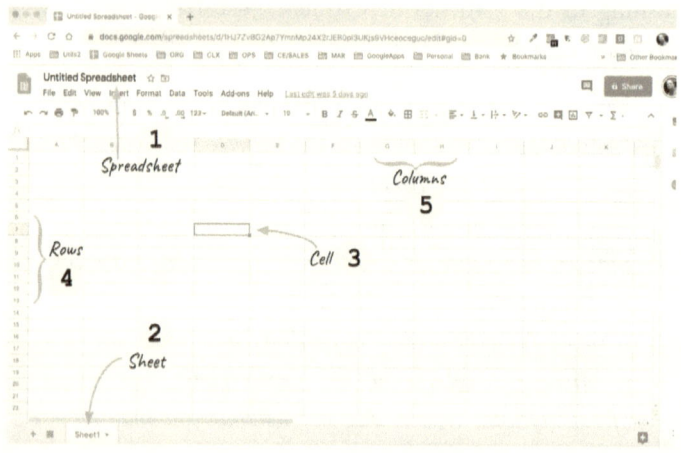

Image: *Google Sheets overview*

It was hard for Jim to consume many pointers, but one thing was clear: "Spreadsheet has got potential and must be immediately implemented".

He started practicing Spreadsheet with intermittent guidance from Verma sir, with a great passion. And soon, developed many tools to simplify his tasks such as a birthday reminder. 'What an awesome tool! Life gonna be fun with this', he whispered.

Life changed after spreadsheet

Now Jim continues to bring smiles on many faces and surprise them on special occasions. And yes, he is getting more bandwidth for his books too. His tools were amazingly helping him maintain the huge data of all the students, friends, staff, and tracking activities of all sorts effortlessly. **Simplified the life is, Happier Jim is!**

Yes, it is bringing smiles to our librarian Mrs. Reena Bhardwaj also, as she doesn't have to maintain manual registers anymore:) :)

Birthday Reminder was renamed as *'Mind the Reminder*'* and shared among many. It was and continues to be an excellent, yet simple infrastructure that could, not only be used for reminding birthdays but also for anniversaries, joining dates, important events for every day, year and lifetime. You get timely notifications on specific dates and times.

It was a one-time effort and life-time benefit with Simplicity, Speed, Data-security and free of cost.

1. Prepare a list of Name, Date of Birth, Anniversary Dates

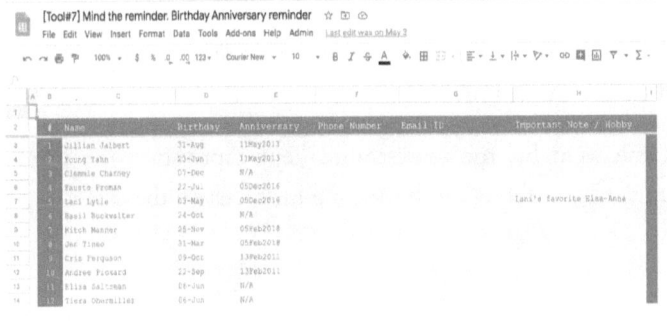

2. Setup for contents and receiver details

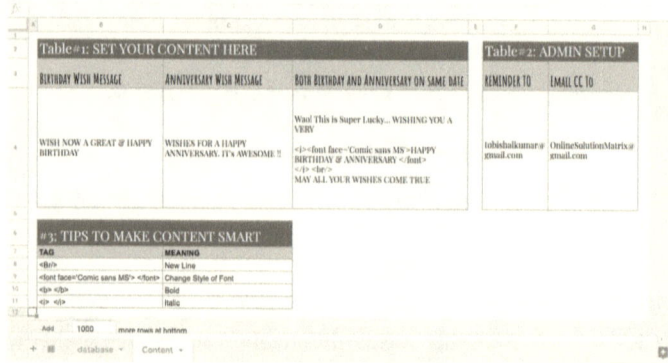

3. Write a few lines of instructions

4. Tell Google to run this instruction at a specific time.

Timely wishes always leave positive vibrations in everyone's heart. This was working wonderfully for Jim, and many still did not know the secrets behind this. Jim also made other systems such as Placement Coordination System (PCS) which helped his classmates and the generations later on. PCS gave a collated view of matrix between a number of companies, offering packages, branches, list of placed candidates, etc into a dashboard that continued to play a vital role in the placement structure in the university.

Time went by, the mastermind kept captivating the whole university without compromising his focus on the career.

|| Recap ||

Fundamental Techniques Towards Preparing Your Own Theory

PRINCIPLE #1
Do whatever comes on your way till you know passion. Enjoy.

PRINCIPLE #2
Identify the core niche that makes you the best version of you.

PRINCIPLE #3
Know that knowledge is just 20%, Implementation is rest 80%.

PRINCIPLE #4
Deep dive into core niche, get the secret sauce.

PRINCIPLE #5
Utilize the resources and people available. Be grateful.

PART TWO

FOLLOW INTUITION, THE TRUTH

Corporate Life Begins

An omen is a phenomenon that is believed to foretell the future, often signifying the advent of change. People in ancient times believed that omens bring a divine message from their god.

Omen is also called portent or presage Turtle? The turtle seen in a dream indicates an unusual improvement, positive. The turtle is a symbol of good fortune and longevity. The turtle is a positive omen bringing 10,000 years of happiness. "Great Turtle — The wisest of all creatures in Iroquois mythology."

Do you remember your feelings before joining your first job, and the heartbeat…? were excited... relaxed or nervous...? :)

Jim was eager to join the world-class MNC believing that it was going to be his dream job, like anybody else in the world.

As a Software Engineer, Life at MNC started with programming, unit testing the modules, and a lot of environment setup, be it Java's Spring-struts or validating the code for performance testing. He was fully enjoying his work which also involved Client meetings, understanding the requirements, listing discussions as MOM, brainstorming with the team and sometimes prolonged sitting at War-room for nonstop work.

Being at MNC he was getting good exposure working with Geo-located teams as they had clients from Belgium, USA, France, etc. A project from France for the Dept. of Building & Security system was really exciting.

Months passed with great enthusiasm, learnings, and in the regular fashion (long meetings, discussing ideas, and explications). He found himself in a world filled with a variety of new tools & technologies – Eclipse, ALM, Struts, Spring Framework, SOAP UI, etc. He was transforming the complete environment with small magical steps; little conscious and mostly lost.

> *Jim is super-excited in collaborating with brilliant minds and getting various opportunities to explore; like he always wanted. Well said, **"As you sow, so shall you reap"**, or the same in other way is also called **"Law of attraction"**.*

A Ritual called "Standup"

One of the things he noticed was that for any team in the organization, the most binding ritual was to have daily standup, which was turning tedious as a few would come late, a few suddenly taking sick leave, and some weren't ready with their updates. Gradually people lost interest or seriousness, and tracking also went for a toss. It was a daily activity followed by preparation of MOM, followup-reminder for all would consume another couple of minutes. It was becoming monotonous and more of a routine for the team, without much value addition.

Jim couldn't resist coming up with a fix for this, and the very next day he came up with a 3-step prototype tool. "Standup management system(SMS)", that covered many aspects to make a meeting focused and traceable. **Simple, inHouse, and more importantly, it was 'Free'**.

SMS was taken as a test launch within the team. This not only helped all the participants with a transparent management system but also concluded their daily standup effectively within 5 to 8 minutes for their eight membered team. Believe it!

Below is a prototype on implementation of SMS tool, a 3-Step Mechanism:

---

* A tool being Free is very important to skip a lot of approval processes.

1. Setup the team [one time]

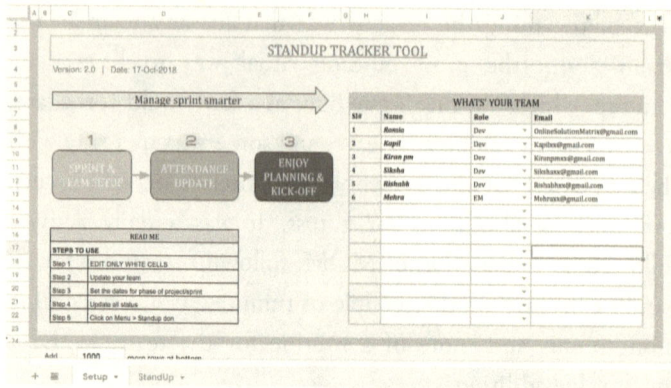

2. Mark the attendance & status-updates during meeting (User-stories, the worklist per member, will be predefined and one-time setup)

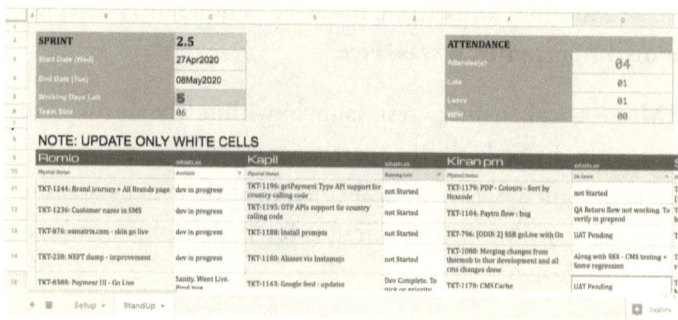

3. Click on menu Admin > StandUp Done

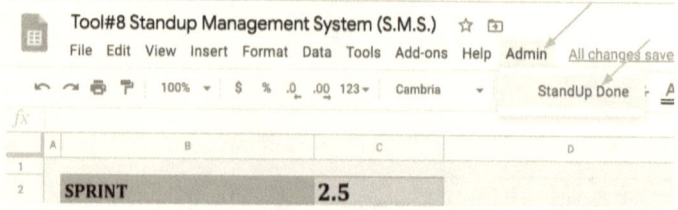

4. Email sent to all team & data archived at another sheet for report

Daily Stand Up | L.A.M. Tech | 03May2020

SPRINT	2.5	ATTENDANCE	
Start Date (Wed)	27Apr2020	Attendee(s)	04
End Date (Tue)	08May2020	Late	01
Working Days Left	5	Leave	01
Team Size	06	WFH	00

* * * * * *

Once Jim's best friend who worked in the healthcare industry was discussing how their meetings went for hours and hours and sometimes without any outcome. His startled eyes remained wide open for seconds, when Jim said how he and his team drove the same in 10 minutes. Jim explained to him about Standup-meetings and its benefits. It had just 3 pointers (in sequence) as below: *What I did **Yesterday**, What's plan for **Today**, and Any **Blockers** or dependency?*

Benefits of using Standup Management System (SMS):

- *It captures and refreshes the day-wise attendance*
- *It creates MOM with pointers on the fly*
- *All the participants can easily update the status*
- *Sends update to all the attendees over the email with just a click*

Being a smart learner, Jim could set himself on those new organisational tools & environments without much difficulty;

Standup tool is accessible at bit.ly/standupTool

which was very impressive for his manager, that's what even his team-lead believed.

He was also recognized for "Employee Achievement Award" twice in the last 6 months.

When it came to Fun activities, his name was not missed there too. He was equally active in other activities like games, music, dance, sports, or anything related to innovation. Foosball was his favorite. If he was not seen around his desk then most of the time he was found pumping power-shots at the Foosball table.

Image: *Foosball*

The days and months were passing happily, what else could one imagine in the initial days of first job or first love.

* * * * * *

With passing time, sometimes he realized that working on so many technologies were keeping him much occupied, but this routine & environment was provoking for something… something was missing!

> *Working on these small modules repeatedly was restricting him & making his job monotonous. "Does life have to be like this?", "Why cannot I become a part of a bigger picture – Working with Elon Musk towards modeling spaceships, Or say preparing rigorously to perform as a superhero role in the next Avengers movie." Contentment was missing.*

A couple of months later, while working on a module for 'Department of Building & Security System' (heard an inner voice as someone was knocking his heart), he got up from his chair, went close to the corner-window, looked outside at the greenery & busy street, and said to himself:

> *"Jim, for how long will you be restricting your energy. Though there are multiple projects with varied potentials, are you getting enough space to look at bigger aspects? Where are you heading Jim? Are you just meant for these."*

All these thoughts started knocking him now & then, here & there. A few weeks continued with the same hazy and noisy voice…

StarNovation – event that innovates

For the next two months, Jim was occupied with a new product release that encroached his weekends. One Friday evening, a mail popped up in his inbox with the invitation for an event, that read:

"Nominate your ideas with STARNOVATION".

Every year, this event is organized to showcase #10 best ideas based on Innovation that would add value to the contemporary business or social structure, out of 100+ nominations. One can develop a product or a prototype, which can either be based on a fresh new idea, or to increase efficiency at work, or maybe something to help the society upgrade their lifestyle.

Innovation! Innovation! and Innovation!

The talk was in the air. Meeting room, Lunch table, HR desk. everywhere.

Everyone on the floor was talking about it except the daemon coder. The HR team was getting aligned with their set of tasks to make it a great success and stand meaningful, with expectation of more than 100 participants.

From planning, registration, maintaining & tracking data, status updates to arranging the materials like posters, danglers, printing certificates, budget for their rewards and the list was long, really long... had to be taken care of by the HR team with support of the Admin.

There was a chance of direct recognition by the CEO for the great ideas. Two of the best was to be honoured with a short trip to Singapore, while two runners up were supposed to get a cheque of INR 1Lac. Since the participant list was long and was from other locations too, "driving it without using a certain software was becoming a mammoth task" , HR head Mary said to her team "We may go out of our mind and time".

Only 10 days were left, Mary and her entire team were going crazy, she was approaching the finance team to buy a software for this and on the other hand pushing the team to brainstorm and find some ways to make the event a real success, "help with some Innovation at HR team first".

The Finance team already had 2 requests from other departments towards soaking-out the available budget, hence not favoring to accommodate Mary's request and was diverting her to the management. She was putting a lot of her energy and time approaching the management, CEO of the organization, but none of her smartness or skills were getting materialized.

Mary's brain was shared to work in 3 directions,

1. One towards following up with management,

2. Other squeezed to bring some tool or online product or event planner to help, and

3. Last part to push people on the floor "Come on guys, we can do it".

Literally, she was disturbed. Mary was everywhere on the floor with her heart & soul. Her eyes sank with dark circles reappearing after a year; not even taking food on time or break for a coffee. She really wished for a Santa to appear from somewhere and gift atleast some solution to her problems.

> *"And, when you want something, all the universe conspires in helping you to achieve it. Paulo Coelho, The Alchemist". (Book top)*

* * * * * *

Only a week was left

> *"Hey! Did you try coffee from the newly installed vending machine?", Naveen asks Mary. "No dear," Mary replies surprisingly. "It has flowery aroma & is absolutely smooth on tongue", he continues. Naveen, the admin guy, has been a coffee lover since he traveled Amsterdam on an official trip.*

Mary stepped out for a coffee with Naveen; fully exhausted… still trying to recall what she has heard about Google App Script in the previous organization, that could be helpful in automating her sheets, but not getting enough clarity or time to start upon.

It was just God's grace that Jim too reached to fill his coffee mug in a hurry, and noticed Mary standing beside the machine, thinking silently and lost. He asked the reason for her frustrated face and if he could offer some help. They both had a quick & refreshing interaction about their past – Hometown, Jim's love for solving puzzles, Mary's previous company, and then suddenly Jim mentioned his "Birthday reminder tool" he made in college days.

"Santa found!", Mary's heart sparkled. For the next few hours, Mary was all over the table, and ***emptied her mind she needed to cook StarNovation lavishly***:

- Ideas come into a repository
- Based on category, acknowledgment and response
- System to collate all inputs
- Follow-up and reminders to participants
- Participation certificates for everyone: Design, Data, & Print – she can create design
- A visual dashboard on status for everyone

Jim came as a Ray of Hope when all were in a turmoil about enduring the event. Now Mary and Jim were meeting regularly and taking this head to head. Jim was excited to help her and the organization. And within 3 days an excellent yet simple tool was ready with every requirement mentioned, and even better.

Below steps take you through Tool creation & execution:

The high-level of the system by Jim, as below:

1. A Google Form to take responses
2. Structure the responses using referencing

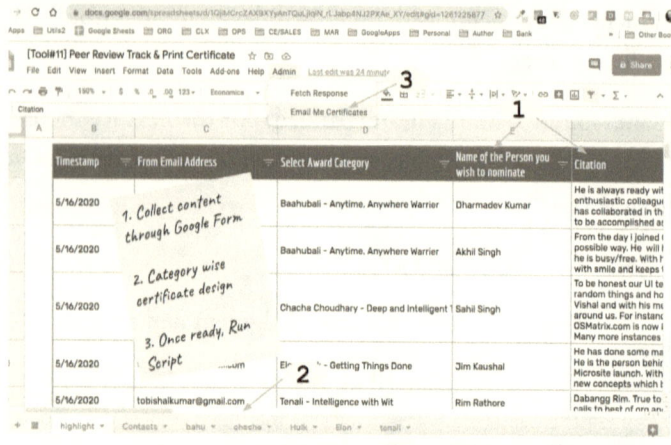

3. Category-wise certificate outline & design on sheets

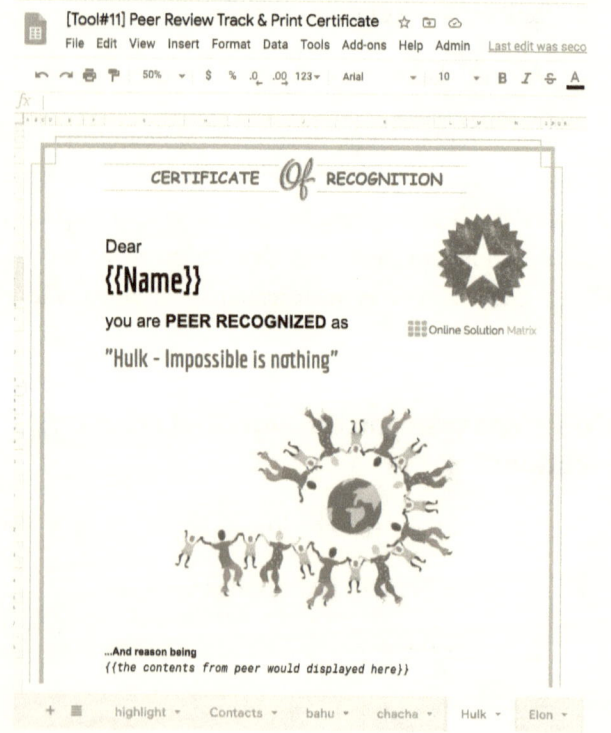

Corporate Life Begins | 61

4. Automated Response system to participants and stakeholders
5. Automated Certificate creation with all data
6. Structured archiving of certificates and automated emails

StarNovation ran for 2 days and was successfully managed with the Power of Spreadsheet (...and Jim). Jim missed the nomination for himself because he was turning the wheel, but assured to leave a mark on everyone's heart, including the participation certificates that people pinned at their workstation.

And Jim too got a wonderful Peer-recognition from the same certificate automation system by the leadership team. :)

---

* To know more about Spreadsheet. Refer the Epilogue after the story

(Many more tools were created on Spreadsheet for other departments & purposes like Quality Assurance, Hiring, Exit, Training & Finance. Jim's remarkable show went on…)

* * * * * *

It's been some days now, with that captivating event was over…

A few days and nights, after that captivating event passed over, went on and on.

Jim was back with enormous energy and some spare time. He was so habituated to put his energy into different buckets, a Job with working on one module was insufficient to contain him. He discussed with his manager that he wanted to join him for team management aspects, or how to switch to business roles so that he could be part of different pictures or any big picture and help the organization. But the answer remained the same "let me discuss with the higher management and get back", cunningly presented in different ways. And that made sense to Jim, nothing wrong, managers were also answerable to their managers, and bound to complete the tasks or achieve goals assigned to them.

Two months later…

The guy with the disruptive attitude strongly felt that he was born to innovate and bring revolution. He started attending workshops, Networking events, Startup sessions of co-working spaces over the weekends.

To make events more productive, he soon started a platform where startup enthusiasts and founders could join, share & solve each other's problems over the table, named it "***Neighpreneur – Meet Neighborhood Entrepreneur***". During this journey, he met 100s of entrepreneurs who were working on some ideas & had challenges of various kinds. Some were struggling to stabilize, some had co-founder challenges (finding a cofounder, or being in sync with), a few were going well but stuck at one-level as they had to be involved in every task to resolve & was not able to come out; while many had just started with no clarity of direction.

The weekends were no more like watching the laughter show for hours or reading a novel sitting on a bean-bag with his favorite coffee mug. Almost every weekend he attended some Meetup with entrepreneurs, listening to their success or failure stories.

Not only these, he also started conducting mentoring sessions and mathematics classes at one of the NGO as a volunteer. NGO, another world full of real beauty and creativity. Wished, he could help many more needy ones.

> *Yes, all these sound like a protagonist from a movie, but trust me this was his real-life that the universe witnessed. Quite similar to college days, just that the scene was changed.*

All these were giving him satisfaction, and strengthening his caliber to manage multiple things, and practicing self-discipline.

Every such action with a positive heart and open thoughts were opening his imagination; and honestly helping others was bringing a new dimension to his life. He was touching many lives with positivity, that was returned by the universe in its own ways.

Despite all that, he experienced a constant inner push to come out of this routined job. A job which was controlling his energies... restricting his spark... **limiting him to tap his true potential.**

* * * * * *

Awakening from all direction

As the time passed, he asked himself, "Are all of these going to stay in a longer run, will I be able to sustain it in future too along with the liabilities coming my way? Inevitable – Finding a life-partner, extending the family, setting the life goals, a good-standard of living, and whatnot."

* * * * * *

There are several factors that ensure that you stay in an organization – timely salary, the environment, the growth opportunities, work-life balance; wherein only one factor is enough to trigger the revolutionary thought of separation – "**Relationship with your Immediate Manager**". Yes right, This one thing of having right relationship with your immediate manager is crucial. While you grow, you have to be the favorite of your manager; there is no doubt in it and those who are good at this, can survive longer.

Managers are crucial in the organization, be it knowing your role in the company, your daily tasks, switching roles or even to understand "Am I needed in the organization ?". Someone has well said, there are only two thumb rules in an organization when you are confused –

Rule #1 – The Boss is Always Right, and Rule #2 – If The Boss is Wrong, See Rule#1.

#MANAGER

> *RULE #1*
> *The Boss is Always Right*
>
> *RULE #2*
> *If The Boss is Wrong, See RULE #1*

Also to understand managers better, they are many times bound to make you do the task which is the need of the hour, rather than what is defined in your KRAs(Key Responsibility Areas) or OKRs(Objectives and key results) during goal settings.

Knowing all of that, one of Jim's friends (who is an author and founder to mid-size company) couldn't resist himself from advising – 'It is always better to put all the energies and thoughts towards one goal, rather than focusing on many. But you need to decide intellectually the path you want to travel in order to succeed'.

> *"10,000 hrs of deliberate practice on same thing can turn you to become specialized from generalized". Credit: According to Malcolm Gladwell's theory*

This piece of text was like an awakening for Jim. His thoughts went deeper & deeper. How to focus on specialization while making a good earning, and not just doing everything.

A call from startup

A month later, during a coding-challenge fest organized at his office, he met Mr Rajeev (the programmer turned full-time entrepreneur), who had been running a firm for nearly 10 months, offered him to join his firm with minimal in-hand salary. And if he joined immediately, he would be offered a Co-founder role as well. Jim was disturbed. He knew the answer but wanted to get his intellect to come along. And this captivating message from Rajeev made a deep-mark on his heart –

> **"Jim, you join now as a co-founder,
> or join me later as an employee".**

Jim and Rajeev had a few more interactions over time and were kind of getting to know each other's journey and of course their potential. In a small corner of his mind, Jim noticed that Rajeev was fond of turtles, be it his key ring, or the welcome gift to new employees. Articles on his LinkedIn popped up with Turtle beliefs & facts across the world. Coincidentally, a close friend gave Jim a crystal-turtle too.

Why was he noticing so many turtles? Was this some signal, or just a coincidence to be ignored!

Image: *Turtles are positive omens across most communities in world*

During their talk, Rajeev also revealed that they are in discussion with few investors and expecting a good amount of funds in coming months. Therefore, they were looking for some young, energetic & courageous entrepreneurs to join hands to take the company to the next level of success. Jim was thrilled-cum-anxious hearing this.

Days were passing by, and it was cutting him like the edge of a sword, he was considering every detail that would help him to take this life changing decision. He also consulted a few of his seniors, mentors in this regard; prepared SWOT analysis and also used the 5-WHYs tool. One day he somehow managed the courage to discuss this with his family, that he was going to leave his well paying job and to begin with an entrepreneurial journey which only ended up with chaos and fear of 'what if startup gets closed'.

* * * * * *

That evening he left the office a little early, tasks were completed as usual. He was almost sliding on lying his head on an old cemented-bench with his head leaning on the support, body tilted at almost 45 degrees backward so his head is resting well, inat a green park besides hind his house. One of his favorite quote was ***continuously chanting chatering*** in his brain, mind, soul and almost everywhere –

> **"A ship in harbor is safe, but that is not what ships are built for."**

Having a safe job with an on-time salary was not something he just wanted to live with.

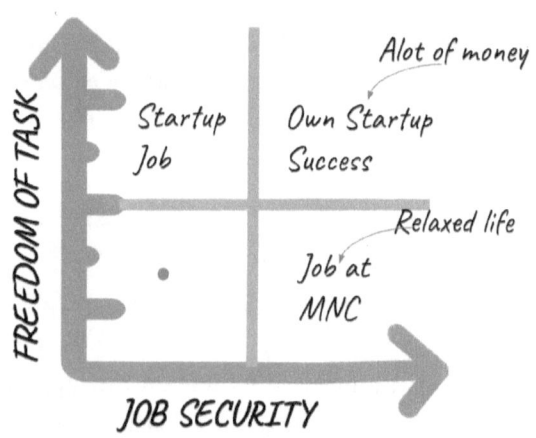

Image: *Four-Quadrants of Job security vs Freedom of task.*

To shut the internal chattering

*The internal chatters are the consistent monologue, every human being, and if allowed to exaggerate, every creature on the planet, plays in their brains. This chatter is ignored by most people, and this internal chatter is what creates the reality of one creature. Believe it or not, It is **playing all the time**, even now when you are reading this. Some chattering examples in below table:*

News	Internal Chatter (few unconscious)
your friend joined a new company	Should I switch too, what am I doing at my job, Let me talk to him and get the experience
husband get promotion	woohoo! we can have bigger apartment, I will go shopping
Boss is changed	Why did he leave? Is he fired or left, who is going to replace him, will my previous work matter to him

Jim came up with "4-step Chatterbox fixing methodology", with experiences over solving this, from college days. And it was similar to product development model(Agile methodology) in his company.

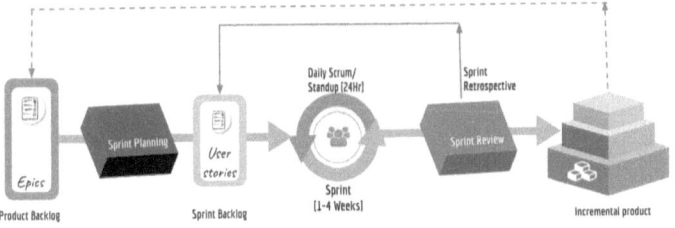

Image: *Scrum, a technology-product development methodology*

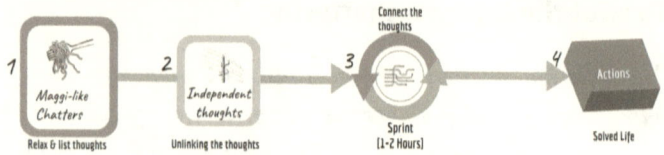

Image: *Chatterbox fixing methodology. Maggi > Wires > Railway joins > Action*

Similar to Scrum (project development method), the first step was to bring all the thoughts into a place.

- List down all the Chatters running wildly.
- Unlink these thoughts
- Spend some time to connect back relevant thoughts and leaving out the random
- Action

After an hour of lonely, solely and calmly sitting in the park, breaking-down all the maggi-like-tangled chatters into independent electricity-cables, and connecting back like the railway-stations where trains meet. Jim was calm & content. His brain, mind, body & even the spirits; were aligned with the choice that was already made by his heart long back.

Ten percent (of the brain) myth

A person's brain determines how they experience the world around them. The brain weighs about 3 pounds and contains around 100 billion neurons – cells that carry information.

According to surveys by renowned psychologists, around 75% of human-kind believe that we only use 10% or less of our brain. But this is just a myth. Science explains clearly that the majority of the brain is almost always active.

1. *If 10 percent of the brain is normally used, then damage to other areas should not impair performance. Instead, Even slight damage to small areas of the brain can have profound effects.*

2. *Brain scans have shown that no matter what one is doing, all brain areas are always active. Technologies such as positron emission tomography (PET) and functional magnetic resonance imaging (fMRI) reveal that even during sleep, all parts of the brain show some level of activity.*

The brain requires up to 20 percent of the body's energy (oxygen & nutrient)—more than any other organ—despite making up only 2 percent of the human body by weight. If 90 percent of it were unnecessary, there would be a large survival advantage towards selection and removal of unrequired brain parts.

Jim took the opportunity and differentiated between the Brain, the Mind, and the Heart:

Brain – Logical; Processes our thought

Mind – Cognitive; The consciousness of having thought

Heart – Emotional sentiments; The Love, Kindness and Care

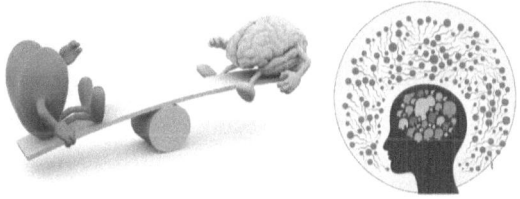

Jim had to listen to all three to make an integrated coordinated team and play well to knock-off bigger games.

* * * * * *

Resignation

[Subject: Resignation Email | Sr. Software Engineer – Jim Kaushal]

Dear Sir,

> *With due regards, I am writing this email to intimate that I have decided to resign from my current designation "Sr. Software Engineer". The reason for this resignation is going for "entrepreneurship", and has been a very thoughtful call.*
>
> *I've learned so many coding techniques, and frameworks (Spring, JSF), which I will certainly take with me throughout my career.*
>
> *I request to be relieved at the earliest possible date.*
>
> *Wishing the company continued success.*

With regards,
Jim Kaushal | Sr. Software Engineer | xxx.xxx.xx41
About Us | Linkedin | Twitter | Facebook

Jim was clear & confident about his decision during his 1-o-1 with the manager. Manager was somehow unexpectedly mum-silent in his approach and conversation that time, while Jim put his points confidently, about joining a running startup, by a guy(with unique idea and future potential), whom he knew very well.

|| Recap ||

Fundamental Techniques on How to Turn Potential into Performance

PRINCIPLE #1
Be honest to your work & people around.

PRINCIPLE #2
Believe on higher energy, than yourself.

PRINCIPLE #3
There are calls from your inner self or universe. Be open to receive.

PRINCIPLE #4
Walking alone in the right direction is better than walking with others in the wrong direction.

PRINCIPLE #5
Take time for yourself daily. Focus on your thoughts. Become Selfish to become Selfless.

||||| PART THREE |||||

THE SEVEN LESSONS TO NOT FAIL IN STARTUP

… The Startup that Burns

The Startup that Burns | 77

What is a startup?

a young company founded by one or more entrepreneurs to develop a new product or service, unique or a variation to existing, and bring it to market.

Startups face high uncertainty and have top rates of failure, but a minority of them do become successful and make others worth giving trial. These few startup become unicorns, implies that companies valued at over US $1 billion.

In Year 2020, Total 11 Indian startups — Unacademy, Pine Labs, FirstCry, Zenoti, Nykaa, Postman, Zerodha, Razorpay, Cars24, Dailyhunt and Glance — became unicorns; few because of the unique challenges that the Pandemic Covid-19 lockdown had presented.

Image: *Usain Bolt after winning his 1st Gold Medal*

Jim and his new partner are working from morning 8am to 10pm at night vigorously. Sometimes even spending an entire night at their new co-working space that they have moved recently. Their experiences and the potentials are giving them wings to fly. **Everyone wants to be successful. We all want to win. But not everyone wakes early, stay late and sacrifice. And not everyone keeps hope till this sacrifice pays off.**

Working for 10 months now, with team size grown from 4 to 34, and the revenue has grown 10-folds. The core 7 departments of any organization was taking its shape here too. Growing this startup "Library for poor" was not an easy cake; but then who wants a simple life, at least not in Jim's dictionary.

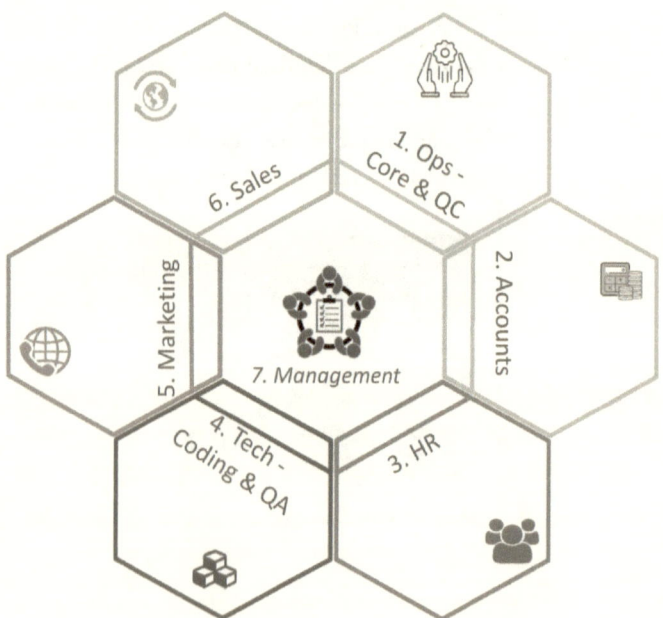

Image: *The 7 Departments of an organization*

The Startup that Burns | 79

Image: *A startup founder is expected to have 10 heads.*

It overwhelms Jim; surrounded with the work that he loves to do, developing his 10 heads avatar – technology revamp, hiring & building a strong team, day-to-day operations challenges, SEO, Branding, UX design, Setting right development culture (Coding & QA), and so on.

Indian mythology is very tricky. One side you see the story, but on the other side, there is a deeper, hidden meaning to every section or character. Ravana's 10 heads symbolize the six Shastras and four Vedas, making him a great scholar and the most intelligent person of his time.

Important note for all who are running or planning for a startup, and looking to create structure – "Understand each department & discuss within the core-members, plus have systems and rituals for each; be it, you may not have a team at the beginning. The long game requires higher preparation and manifestation."

What most of us miss is to have a "***Management***" division. Management is the fluid to connect and flow across all departments and must have its decorum and to think-louder on the vision, revisit the goals, and are the departments in sync with vision? Somehow we miss the sense of seriousness and end up deferring the plan; leading to dilution of actual vision. We are a leader, we must lead.

Quality is the fuel

Through his journey at MNC, one thing was apparent; People overuse the word "Quality", however they miss the actual essence of it. He dived into reading on Quality, studying the great Gurus – be it Philip B. Crosby, Juran, Feigenbaum, Fleming, or Walter Shewhart; on transforming countries and corporates, that will play a key role for the success of a startup. How several companies like Toyota, grew up by implementing quality principles like Six Sigma, kaizen, Poka-yoke, PDCA (Plan Do Check Act).

Jim, a Senior Architect & a Quality head during a discussion –

Jim: First and Foremost, Quality is a **perception** with no absolute measure. It must be defined only in terms of customer satisfaction. Quality begins with a deeper understanding of **who** the users will be, and how & where the product will be **used**. Without such user orientation, good quality is not possible, and It is management's task to translate the current and future needs of customers into products and services.

Senior Architect: "Great, it makes sense. How do we put this into practice?"

Jim: "The above explanation can be translated into two dimensions:

1. External – Customer requirements

2. Internal – Building the product or service correctly

Once you define the requirement, quality is nothing but the conformance to the requirement and one can take judicial based on whether we meet the criteria."

Jim & Architect both were startled when Quality head, demonstrated how "Quality is Free". "More you put efforts into improving quality at initial phase, it will pay much more for itself by

- developing a product that is defect-free (doing first time right).
- saving the humongous reworks.
- adhere to requirements. client satisfaction.
- Example: Say, there is x-amount and y-effort invested in initial phase into Quality; then it is a proven inference that much more of revenue is saved by the defects **not** found, the reworks not required, and the deliverables are much better adhering to client requirement. Though this big ROI(Return on investment: _____) doesn't get measured, as the evaluation of defects, reworks or last minute meetings never come into the picture. Unaccountable."

Jim:

"Each person or stage can be seen as two sides of same coin and coin itself:

- Consumer – to previous stage
- Supplier – to its next stage
- Process

There is no ultimate end point, even the Ideation or consumption to be stepped-back and seen as a stage. Life & Brain is the ultimate creation of God!

For the product industry, Stages would be product design to the programmer, from Quality Assurance to the final user; and the stage for itself will be a process. Similar for the service industry, From Service design to Ops to Quality control to final client deliverable; each stage has 3 roles – consumer, supplier & process."

Credit: *3-role model. (Dr. Joseph Juran in the 1950s)*

Architect:

"I am so thrilled. But I fear this enlightenment would remain as a theory, without getting implemented."

Jim:

"Yes, Knowledge is a pleasing part, but when it comes to implementation, team may find it boring and even unnecessary. I will freely admit this. Please see this as a worthy step of short-term pain for a big value add to long-term gain. A team or individual will always feel discomfort when installing incorporating a new habit, be it Quality or Fitness or Eating healthy."

"It's sort of breaking in a fresh pair of spikes (track shoes) – at first, you may find it alien, but soon they fit like, how were you living without it. Such pain is often a messenger to personal growth. Do not fear or get sluggish. Instead, embrace it."

Image: *spikes may be alien, but then fits to make you win.*

Architect & Quality head together:

"Well, this sounds great. Let's plan for our respective teams on installing incorporating this worthy new habit."

Apart from a detailed session to all employees, Jim ensured to have pictorial banners at office walls. Cultures and discipline are the hardest part, be it an organization or individual, and hence few things have to be repeated till it becomes a part of one's habit.

Spreadsheet, a counter-strike game

Nevertheless, many **utilities** that Jim was building from his favorite handy toolkit "Spreadsheet", saving million bucks, stress, invaluable time in development & setup, and without sharing confidential & personal data to 3rd parties or plug-ins.

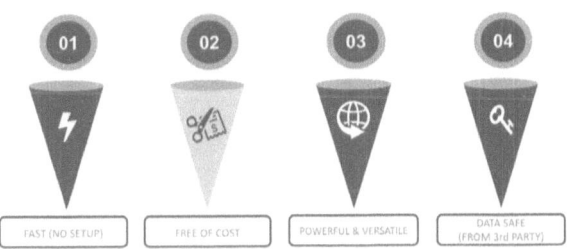

Image: *Benefits with usage of Google Sheets & G.A.S.*

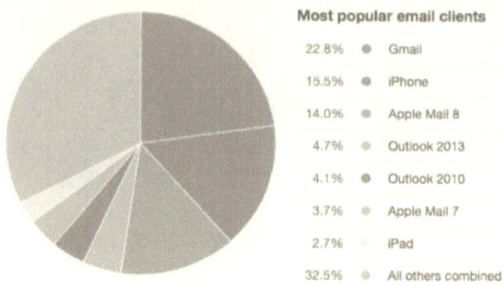

Image: *Email Clients based on "Subscriber opens an email" sent with Campaign Monitor*

Credit: *www.campaignmonitor.com*

The more he explored, the more he got to know about it – Shortcuts, hidden features & more features. The spreadsheet was just endless, like a few games which you keep playing more, and you will get to know more with enhancing speed as a game-player. *"They take minutes to learn, but a lifetime to master"*

BEING AN EFFECTIVE LEADER IS ENORMOUSLY COMPLEX. IT REQUIRES A GREAT VISION, MASTERY TO HAVE GREAT RESOURCE, AND COURAGE FOR UNSTOPPABLE DREAM.

SSS

The Townhall that left the crowd speechless

Whether it is a startup or a stable company, a common objective to look-at is to keep everyone connected towards the company's vision. We get so involved in our daily chores that we miss our actual goal – be it individual or the organization. And the definition of Success shouldn't be mistaken that it means only the Organization's growth or vice versa; instead, it is a combination of both. In short, everybody must grow progressively.

Being a startup, it becomes important to keep every employee aligned with the company's goal. Therefore, he plans for a townhall meeting. Being the co-founder Jim had the privilege of calling a meeting at short notice and so he did. Despite his tight schedule, a calendar invite was sent – "**4pm Townhall**".

From preparing a **compelling pitch** to a **motivational message**, from sharing business potential to company's growth, from coordination with Rajeev on dialect, to welcome-note for new joiners; all were getting added to his checklist (To-Do).

It is Wednesday 10am, a calendar invite pops-up for all 34 members.

* * * * *

All were getting set for the townhall wherein his partner Rajeev, was in a different world. He was performing a unique act altogether. The company was going through a fund-crisis from 3months, which was never discussed with Jim. Rajeev was in belief that sooner or later, he would receive the fund, and the same was told to Jim during his joining. However, there was no context setup thereafter, and Jim believed that it was being taken care.

Image: *Office clocks 12:15pm*

Same day, 12:15pm. Partner Rajeev comes to Jim and reveals something… Something out of last imagination…

"Jim, I want to share something very crucial. Please be calm and listen to me till I am finished with saying. **There is zero cash (yes literal zero, he said) left in the company's Bank Account.** Implies, the situation is so bad that we don't have enough money even to pay this month's salary," and burbled all details.

The investor (highly paid professional) who was an elder brother of Rajeev's friend, working in the US, had committed 40 Lacs INR. He was postponing from few months, and now finally declined with the reason mentioned as his layoff and personal challenges at his end.

It stunned Jim…

"Let us not keep them in dark, let's announce it today to the team," Rajeev said.

Jim could not believe what he just heard, couldn't respond or react.

He was sitting on his chair for the next 2 hrs and in most deep pain, asking himself

"Why didn't I bother to get involved in finance and check the company's bank account"

"Why didn't I ask for the bank statement?"

"Why Rajeev didn't mention himself about such a critical situation, before"...

A big lesson, the hard way, that he missed the thumb-rule of entrepreneurship:

"A co-founder must proactively understand & get updates for all departments, be it far away from his comfort zone"*; and Jim, standing in the darkest tunnel, overlooked the most important aspect of a business, called "Finance".*

He made sure that a cofounder should be into complementary domain or mindset, still missed that business partner should be either one's own blood or a childhood friend whom you know very well (with whom you can share even your undergarments), or someone well-tested*.

Lost in Battle

Jim is clueless. His heart is sobbing and filled with regret for such a decisive mistake from his side. Jim was crying for the second time in his life. (Previously at the farewell ceremony of his sister just after her marriage. Sister, who used to understand

---

* To Test a human, one should try one or more of these 3 options: Game, Fight, or Money transactions.

Jim more than himself & preached invaluable lessons of life. His sister was one who taught that friendship is about understanding the unspoken and should not have expectations attached. Jim was only fifteen then). He finds himself helpless with regret for the cosmic mistake that he made. The heart was beating faster than ever, and blood circulating through all the brain-cells in his head, that **what now...?**

The 4PM townhall took place.

In place of Jim, his partner took the lead.

Instead of the company's growth & business potential, Fund-crisis was announced.

In place of message on building strong team & stay focused, a piece of terrifying news was spread.

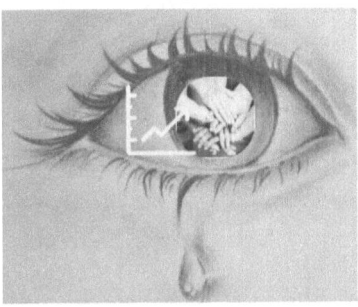

Image: *Drop of tears rolled out from eyes with dreams and plan*

The townhall that turned into a fearful stage.

The townhall that left everyone shattered.

...the townhall that made the Co-founder cry!

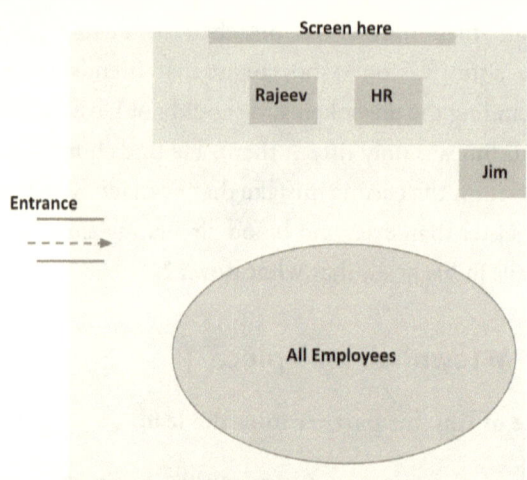

Image: *The meeting hall*

Jim took a corner place next to the podium. His partner made the announcement & explained the circumstance. Everybody in the hall went in absolute silence after hearing. "We are extremely sorry to say that there is No funds left to continue the operations, we have to exit". Jim was also asked to address the team, but he was speechless; hardly able to make eye-contact with anyone. Somehow he took the courage, stepped forward but uttering any word was hard. And all he could say was, "Sorry"… and another "Sorry" in a shivering tone… and tears rolled out.

Townhall ended abruptly, with no questions asked at that moment. And how could they, when their hero himself was carrying elephant-sized disappointment!

Employee makes a company, Deed makes life

If you hire people based on skills just because they can do a job, they'll work for the salary. But if you hire based on a belief and show trust in their powerful will, they'll work for you with heart and soul.

Admin staff "Soumya" stepped up, voluntarily to put in her personal funds, with a gentle note that "Sir, I have little & not sure how much it will help, but want to come forward to support with possible funds, so the company keeps running". They created moments with such actions when there were no expectations. Though appreciable but couldn't work as Jim was totally a broken piece of heart.

Company was shut in the next 2days with paying off whatever possible. This was the toughest time that any entrepreneur can ever see in his life. The table in the conference room, the black chair in his cabin, all are getting sold. The post-it stickers in meeting rooms, those notebooks in the cabin are still lying on the table, are giving birth to nostalgia for this and the next life for Jim.

> *"Good decisions come from experience, but experience comes from Bad decisions. This is life, so don't worry about however big are mistakes. Go ahead and learn from them."*
>
> *– Credit: Dr. APJ Kalam.*

With bringing consciousness back, in this hard time Jim was extending support to his employees in all the ways – by connecting them with different firms & startups within his network. Also, he emphasized manpower consulting firms to help out.

It took a few days to stabilize his emotional spikes. A large iceberg had hit the titanic ship; big, sudden, unseen.

Life without job

It feels shit to not have a job!

Jim, a dreamer, a mastermind is without job and impatient to do actions. Should he join a fresh vision; or should he work on his own idea?

Instead, Jim is taking time to identify his actual existence, and his real trait. This hard time is taking him through various aspects of life. He started saving every single buck possible, Survival became tough at a point that sometimes had free food (prasadam) at a temple to skip his lunch, and few other times skipped. Living with no money was way too hard than reading or listening. He had to think twice even before buying his favorite Rs. 15 Egg-Puff* and Tea.

Image: *(i) Those outlets having delicious snacks.*
(ii) Egg-puffs with tea (INR 40 for 2pcs)

A feeling of emptiness, erupting of weird random thoughts in the mind; those are hard to express to anyone; This was happening with Jim for the very time and the experience is worth

---

* *Egg puff – Egg wrapped within a crispy layer of flour, sold at street outlets.*

mentioning. Several conflicting thoughts kept on banging hard, one set of thoughts made regretful, guilty, and untrustful and the other made self-awaken, decisive, mindful, and conscious.

Soon he realizes that it is also important that one should have No job sometimes.

So he turns to the other side of life and realizes that it is also important that '*Doing Nothing is so important for self-realization and self-cleaning,* 'as it enables us to do & learn certain things that we don't pay attention to while being in the race of life.'

Two weeks passed like that...

He was fortunate to connect with a mentor to clear his mind and guide the one-path; the one-path that is always there, and usually unrecognized by oneself. And you just need a right word and rest things start falling in place. Same happened to Jim.

A mentor is a guru who relishes, enjoys seeing the growth of his mentee with time and in a manner that suited his/her talent the best.

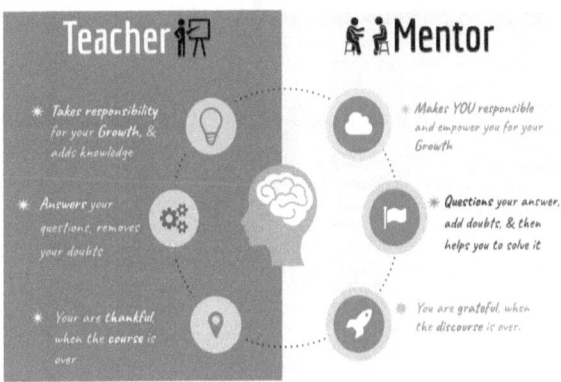

Image: *Teacher and Mentor in your life*

Jim was easily able to map the differences between his loving teachers from the past and Morpheus of Matrix, a Hollywood movie, who just showed up at the perfect time. *"While a teacher takes responsibility for your growth; Mentor makes you responsible & empowers you for your growth. Teacher believes in transactions(learning), while Mentor believes in transformation"*.

Jim started exploring skills that would be perpetual. Knowledge that would retain with him throughout life:

- techniques of self-analysis,
- workshop for emotional intelligence & emotional fitness,
- 7-days mastery on how to adapt & improvise; and
- one greatest skill: how to learn a new learning

Affirmation Jim used to work on Self-control:

I am patient in every scene and handle it with calm and ease.

I admit my fault, apologize, accept responsibility, and change.

I get over the guilt and release the past, I focus on rebuilding my relationship.

I have the discipline and will-power to be Self Sovereign and create a destiny of my choice.

|| Recap ||

7 Lessons to NOT FAIL as Leader

PRINCIPLE #1
Do not stick to your tasks and department. Get out of comfort zones.

PRINCIPLE #2
Do not leave any journey of your business uncovered. Cover end-to-end by yourself.

PRINCIPLE #3
Do not find partner whom you met recently and/or who is like you(Skills).

PRINCIPLE #4
Do not miss to plug-in the Quality(mindset) from beginning. Quality is Free!

PRINCIPLE #5
Do not miss to allocate time to find & meet Mentor.

PRINCIPLE #6
When it comes to Finance, until Amount is not in Bank Account, they are NOT.

PRINCIPLE #7
Do not be aggressive or reactive to People. Be supportive even during exit.

||||| PART FOUR |||||

HOW TO SETUP A WINNING BUSINESS

A New Beginning from Scratch

Airbnb is valued at over US$38bn. At times, they had plenty of listings on the site, and plenty of site traffic – but too few bookings. The co-founders grabbed their camera and went to knock on doors-on-doors, persuade the owner & take a ton of photographs of the inside for them to upload. Within a month of starting this strategy – sales doubled. Then tripled. Then....well, the rest is history.

Toyota finely-honed production processes were so efficient and lean that they were able to beat US car makers at their own game from 82% to mere less than 50%. In the world of manufacturing, Toyota is pretty much the grandfather of exactly 'continuous improvement'.

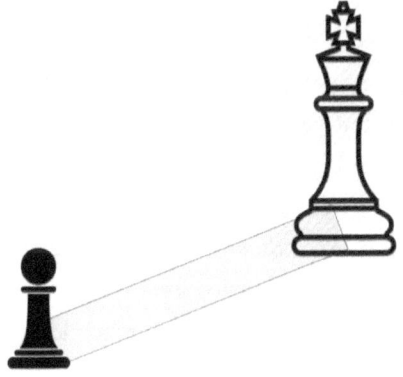

Strategy is a plan of action designed to achieve a **long-t**erm or overall aim.

Jim Kaushal has been practicing self-realization through meditation, and chanting the Gayatri mantra – a 32 syllable sacred incantation (taught in early life by his parents). This used to set up a perfect resonance in his body, mind and spirits; and brought lots of positivity. Thus, despite all external chaos, he continued with peace in mind and harmony to resonate with the inner world.

It was 4:30 early in the morning. He was restless and experienced some unknown sound or calling that made him hard to follow or focus. Jim came out of his bed and to his best conscious state of mind, started uttering Gayatri mantra with closed eyes; well tutored to most of the children in the Indian middle-class families. He felt a divine energy (like **omens**) giving a message – "You will find a delightful surprise today". Calm.

Search for the break

Jim had a strong college alumni network, and that took him a step ahead during his hardship. He was meeting with fresh ideas and people every day, and this time he made sure that there is a high weightage to deeper frequency alignment with the idea and the person. Just an innovative idea, a good-hearted team, and the potential market were not enough. He listed the four paths and started knocking-off point by point. Taking a job at MNC, and landing into a middle-line manager, was first to be taken off the list.

1. Fresh start-up from list of own ideas

2. Join as co-founder to another startup

3. Mid-sized startup with funds & value-adding idea

4. Join back to MNC

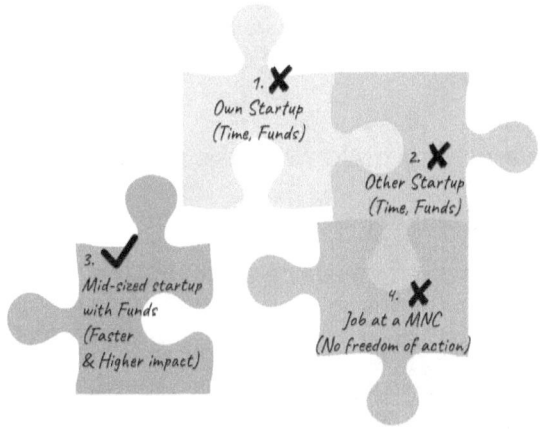

Image: Best option selection

He has been happily solving problems irrespective of domain, department or limits. Every organization needs some technical skills, good communication, various experience, but none of the JD (Job description) said – "Looking for executioner who can take the company to next level", "Fast learner towards getting things done – be it sales, business strategy, coding, QA, operations or hiring"

He attended a few events & seminars including the co-founders meet. Met multiple founders who were looking to start a new venture after their last startup failed. Some of them, including Jim himself, reflected on what they learned from that, and what they would do differently, the next time around. Yet, there were many for whom failure was extrinsic. Perhaps, they picked the right idea at a wrong time or didn't receive the backing from investors at the right time, or they didn't have the right co-founder. Perhaps this, perhaps that. The reasons were endless…

Whatever be the reason, the focus on self-reflection and what more could have been done within the control should not be deflected.

Visionary, King-maker and the meeting

Mr. Rohit Chadha is a 5'6" whitish complexion guy in his mid-40s, and from the same college as Jim. He has just returned from the UK after an on-site of 10 years & his part-time business "LAM Technologies" which is waiting to jump on the next level. He is straightforward to speakup that he has earned sufficient and need not to worry for a livelihood in this life. His idea of business is to create a change in this planet by creating opportunities in multiple dimensions. News about the failure-exit of Jim's startup reached him too.

Chadha and Jim met over coffee at the nearest CCD, having less crowd as usual. They spent almost six hours (continuous) to make logical-connect to the choices they have made. Four empty glasses of coffee piled up with 2 plates of the crispy Potato wedges, and too busy to finish that as the conversation kept their whole mind & heart occupied. Jim maintained his voice note and frequency in a more controlled fashion.

The Meeting of Jim and Rohit was so resonating & making sense to both; it was like Chetak (the horse) meeting Rana Pratap[*]; and Dragons meeting Queen Daenerys.

---

[*] (Refer Images from Author's diary for further reference.)

Taken from a very famous poem and historic mention about a powerful & loyal horse; who used to be in a ultimate state of synchronization with his king 'Rana Pratap'

Image: *Chetak with Rana Pratap, Queen Daenerys from Game of thrones*

Jim took Mr. Chadha through his exciting & adventurous journey of life, offering thick & thin layers with several learnings & lessons. He also shared a few of those wonderful tools developed by him for fulfilling job tasks and early startup requirements.

For Chadha, this was much more than tools creation – It was the intention to solve real-time challenges, it was about indulging & helping people irrespective of borders (department) and communities. All these were sounding enough to trigger the spark of extreme confidence. He could sense the real potential with 'Never Give up' attitude in Jim.

Chadha Sir was into an impressive note, and could sense the real potential in Jim. The long discussion finally ended with a handshake and a win-win situation for both. They looked positive & confident to take the game together.

First catchup and reborn

"Legal Alphabets Matrix (LAM) technologies was all set to add a new dimension to the universe of the Legal-tech industry". Mr. Chadha continued "Today we are selling-buying almost everything over the internet; be it groceries, shoes, medicines, insurances, cars, and even our inner-wear; but the legal industry where most of the work is done on papers is yet an untapped market. No single versatile brand is available for the common people to onboard."

The two major divisions of LAM technologies

1. Services
2. Product

Both of these will be serving both domains –

1. Litigation (Direct legal actionable) and
2. Non-Litigation (Intervention of Court not required).

It is the need of hour, reason – "Not a single player in the market is giving a digital platform for all the legal services – Agreement, Government Stamping, Documentation, Legal translation, Affidavit, Notary, Power of Attorney, Annexures."

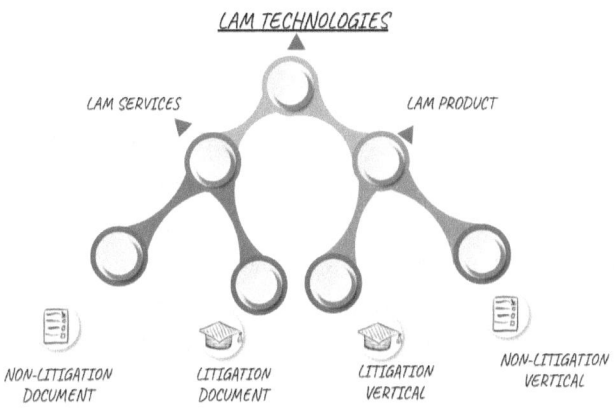

Image: *Org structure for LAM Technologies*

Rohit Chadha was the best idealist that Jim has ever met in his life. The imagination backed by data and confidence made Jim's heart like a jumping jack, thrilled to turn each word into reality on the ground. With heart stroking faster than usual, there was a sound sense of relief; a rare-combination before a big change in life. A calmness like this Jim never felt before in his life. An enlightening for a new and big venture coming ahead.

"The two most important days in your life are the day you are born and the day you find out why." -Mark Twain

Law of Attraction & Need

Rohit Chadha's imagination, charismatic persona & influencing skills; and Jim's positive attitude, intense energy, & ability to make things happen with a structured approach will be an example that the world will witness soon. Chadha sir was a complete-package of gifts & perfect complementary partner – visionary, financial leveraged, ability to portray; that Jim could have asked from his secret Santa.

"Human beings are excellent at imagination, collaboration and communication. At the same time, we are bad at repetition, compliance and following a system. These are the areas where entrepreneurs use technology to make a difference". A trade-off was naturally created – Jim to own the execution part, while Rohit Chadha to bring the vision & validation. It came up so naturally, as the personal traits were well perceived & accepted.

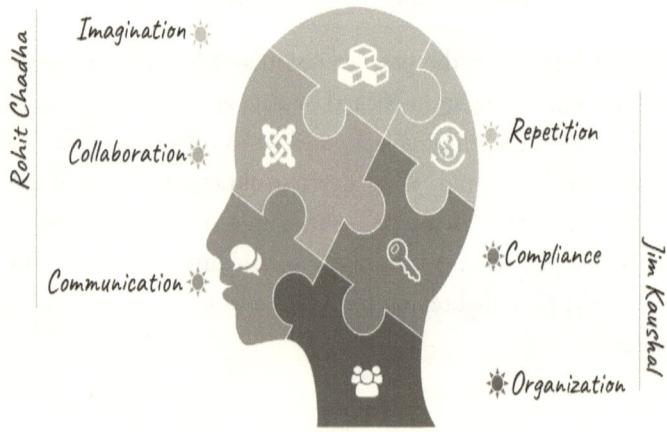

Rohit chadha owned the traits as Imagination, Collaboration & Communication; while Jim Focused on setting up rest of the world – Organization, Compliance and Repetition(towards process automation).

Practise: Do you know your traits, let's have a quick assignment?

Step #1: Rate yourself on below traits:

TRAIT	DESCRIPTION	RATE YOURSELF [5 = OUTSTANDING]	REASON FOR THIS RATING
Imagination	Ability of forming new ideas or concepts not present to the senses.		
Coordination	Ability to work with people smoothly and efficiently		
Communication	Ability to exchange information		
Repetition	Ability of repeating without loss of value or quality		
Compliance	Action of complying with command		
Organization	Ability to organize group of people (with system) for a purpose		

Step #2:

1. Filter out the top scoring traits
2. Identify 5 problems in your current role and capacity
3. Visualize how you can fit your top-traits to solve the above problems

* * * * * *

Role & departments

Jim Kaushal a.k.a. **Jee** (as being called spontaneously by Chadha Sir) will be acting as co-founder and taking charge of complete business (all 6 departments). Jee can take all the necessary actions and do anything that is required for the growth of business, while Rohit Chadha would take charge of market study, product requirement, prioritization of relevant services, and above all the investment & financial decisions. Jee was ensured to have visibility on financials. Within a few minutes of thought restructuring, Jee came up with all department names, and an additional department "R&D".

Rohit chadha specially emphasized on two words – one, being **Accountable**; and second, being **Proactive** on sharing and pulling for insights.

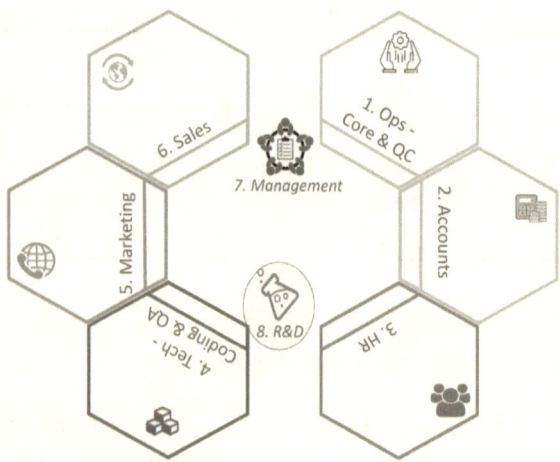

They met routinely after research, more content and deeper thoughts, which marked continuous improvement with each discussion. **Kaizen** in its full action.

1. Operations (OP)

The OP department is the core-heart of an organization where the actual transformation takes place – plastics turns into toys, cotton into textiles, steel into cars. Operations at LAM has to do everything required on ground.

- ◊ Identifying legal service providers on central-level (Company registration, Aadhar Card, etc.) and city level (Notary, Passport Seva Kendra, Panchayat blocks, etc.)

- ◊ Identifying City-level heads for Affidavits, Property legal audits.

- ◊ Identifying the right location for offices where city-head and few employees can sit together to serve direct customers & branding.

- ◊ Onboard distributors in bulk for faster expansion of business

2. Accounts (AC)

AC department records accounts-payable and receivable, monthly financial statement, payroll, fixed assets, taxes and all other financial elements, along with the company's financial position and strategies to run the organization cost-effectively. Good to list the actionables as:

- ◊ Immediate opening of *two separate bank accounts*:

- ◊ Surplus funds account (SFA): Surplus account, with a minimum balance would be 5 times OP running cost, suggested to be 36 months i.e. 3 Years surplus.

And the team must ensure that the balance in SFA is above the minimum. In case it touches the minimum, something seriously has to be worked upon, notify the co-founders and core members – **"Ring the bell as soon it is going to be touched" (please explain)**.

- ◊ Runway funds account (RFA): Account for the Runway cost and daily transactions. All business happens on this RFA. Preferable to have more than one RFAs with different banks and benefits.

- ◊ *Petty cash tracker* (PCT): To track petty cash by different departments for clarity.

- ◊ *Payables*: To collect supplier invoices & expenses.

- ◊ *Payroll*: To collect time worked, as well as pay rate information from HR, tax estimation and other deductions from employee pay, and makes net payment to employees

Yes, All the above, including Petty cash track could simply be created in a simple spreadsheet tracker with proper header, and conditional dropdowns to be shared with stakeholders.

3. Human Resources (HR)

Jim underlined – HR is going to be the most important department. Without **right-fit or set** of employees, the company would just be in a shit. One wrong hiring can lead to devastation and one perfect hiring can share shoulders making LAM the world's best company.

The high-level buckets would be:

- ◊ **Hiring and Recruiting:** Identify, recruit, screen, interview and onboard till immediate manager takes over.

- ◊ **Training & Career plan:** Creates training programs with the help of managers in various departments for new hires and existing employees.

- ◊ **Employee Relations, Compensation & Benefits:** HR handles employee payroll and ensures employees are paid **accurately** and on time, with correct deductions, pension provisions, and other fringe benefits by the employer. Apart from relations and financial pays, compensation also includes benefits like health insurance and free checkups.

- ◊ **Legality:** Interpreting and enforcing various legalities, like employment laws, labor laws, and sexual harassment legislations for the benefit of employees.

    Jim's flat owner once said – "One has already lost the basic purpose of human existence, if he or she is not ethical, moral, or legal"; a lesson that helped in selecting new employees)

The first step for the HR department would be to hire 7-10 key roles, as a strategic hiring based on salary and Employee Stock Ownership Plan (ESOP).

ESOP: When a company gives you equity as part of your compensation package, they're offering you partial ownership of the company. However, your stock/ESOs usually have to vest first, meaning you typically need to work for a period of time before you get the equity. (Vesting is the process of earning an asset across a time period. Refer diagram below).

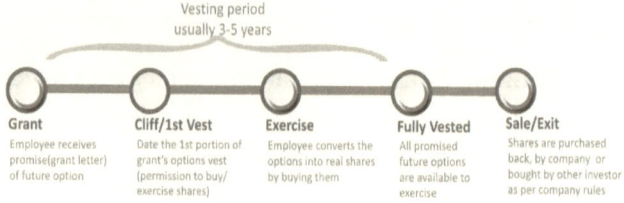

Image: ESOs terminology for the core members

The ESOs will fall into either of 3 categories, based on way & ownership it will be taxed: incentive stock options (ISOs), non-qualified stock options (NSOs), and restricted stock units (RSUs).

4. Technology (TE)

Technology performs the core play game in placing the right system, and then becomes the platform for tons of services, millions of daily transactions & trillions of users active on its chest. Jim ensured to hire a QA team with the right mindset early to exhibit more power for callout and raising voice.

5. Marketing (MA)

Marketing team would create, introduce & maintain position for the LAM brand by promoting the LAM product and services. Brand of the company must be clear & seen undoubtedly as the foremost asset. (Handled by Chadha sir)

6. Sales (SA)

Sales helps the prospect to move through a purchase decision.

*"Marketing gets you a **conversation**, while Sales make the **conversion**"*

7. Management (MG)

Management is an overused term and Jim knew that if this department is not formed and maintained assertively; there will be no *engineering* proceedings at the Organization level. There should be ritual and discipline that is to be followed within this department

- ◊ one-to-one with department heads
- ◊ Mapping Org vision with goals of all departments & keep visiting at intervals
- ◊ "The Why Part" is clearly explained to everyone
- ◊ Inter-department communication is encouraged

A 2 hour weekly meeting scheduled for all the senior leaders to talk on the above agenda.

8. R&D (RD)

The Success Manifestation – Innovation house. Many people, including leaders get this wrong that R&D is about those chemistry labs, or dedicated rooms with special personalities, monetary expenses on setup. Rather R&D is a platform to give the employee (s) a break from their routine tasks and allow the brain to flow multidirectional towards innovation. A place without manager, without boundaries of thoughts.

Jee explained that "R&D will be about spending 2 hours per week (with a flow and structure around), to discuss a new service line and product feature that is not thought ever by LAM technologies or anyone in the world. R&D mainly focuses on quality of thoughts by employees, leaving aside, all the concerns like available team size or funds.". "It is very important to establish a link between the management and R&D discussions to achieve longer sustainability", Mr Chadha added.

9. M.D.T. Communication system

...and this was among the most important COMMON ACTION-GUIDE across departments.

Three steps for a fullproof and powerful communication system. Jim named it MDT Communication System:

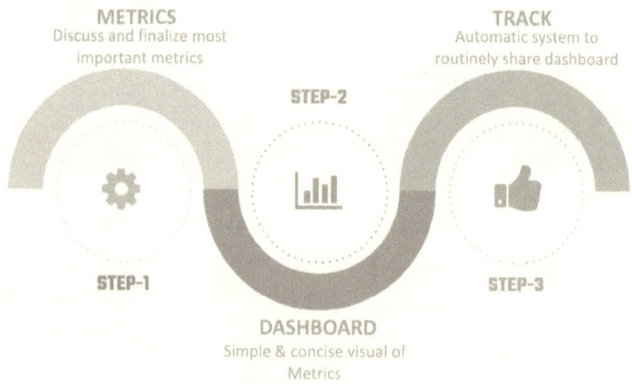

Image: *MDT framework*

9.1 METRICS (M)

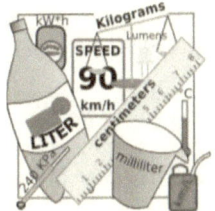

Metrics is a set of numbers that give information about process or activity. Right Metrics and intelligence on Metric-range is crucial to be identified for effective communication & early success.

* LAM's Marketing Metrics: Incremental Sales, SEO Keyword Ranking, Social Sentiment, Web Traffic, Customer Acquisition Cost

* LAM's Sales Metrics: Sales Growth – New and Existing, Average Profit, Conversion Rate, Average Lead Response Time

9.2 DASHBOARD (D)

A simple visual of metrics with quantity, change measurement and special colors or triggers if something outside limits.

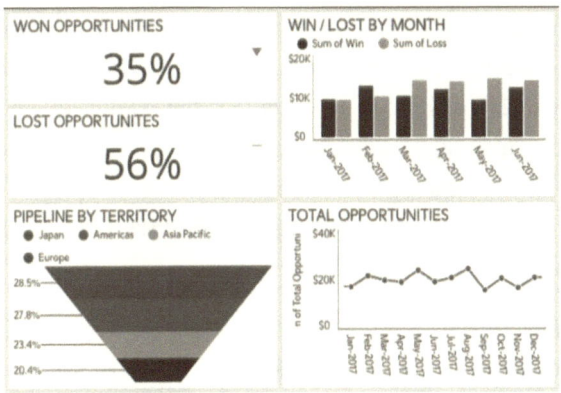

9.3 TRACK (T)

The dashboard must be tracked through a Manual or Automated system; and visited routinely along with team or individually as relevant.

Importance of a co-founder & how to pay

Like a fractal, a startup is an aggregate mirror of its founders' priorities; their ethics, motivations, and philosophies. All these attributes firmly ingrain company's culture and strategy.

*Fractal: Each **Smaller** part of shape has the same character as the **Parent**.*

Image: *Fractal – Smaller parts has same character*

After a little thought and high belief, Chadha sir came up with a compensation package that should not be less and suitable to the financial longevity. He knew that Jim would need to stay awake many nights thinking about the right problems, and there can be nothing more harmful for the company if he is concerned about paying bills and dealing with the associated resentment that he is not paid enough..

Jee was offered 30% of company shares, vested over an expansion of 4 years, and a take home of INR 50k to begin with. Take home would be revised in range 0%-25% with progressive growth of the company, once or twice a year. There would be a notice period of 45 days by either party before final termination of this agreement. Rohit Chadha was taking the bigger risk w.r.t. financial and the ideation part with 60% equity, while the rest of 10% was kept aside, as non-reducible equity for the employee pool.

* * * * * *

Rima paul – 13th Employee

Two months completed since the revamping of LAM **technology**. She was 24th candidate for the interview round for this crucial job opening. Every candidate's details were recorded and tracked into a system with role and feedback; and this was available to the core team before the new candidate was included into the system. **Rima** was in business attire, white shirt with red pencil skirt, along with white heels; which went perfect with her slim figure. "Rima" was a new generation girl with confidence flowing in her every word and action.

Image: *Rima's classy outfit on the first day*

Jim was very calculative & selective when it came to hiring an employee, and ensured the same while interviewing Rima. After four rounds, including Mr. Chadha's one-on-one, she was hired as "HR Head". Till HR was finalized, All the HR stuff and maintenance were done by Jim. A startup is an entity formed to search for a repeatable and scalable business model, towards becoming an organization.

For a startup, It is very important that co-founders walk the journey themself – doing initial tasks, repeat, identify must-have and good-to-have, create a framework, and then hire the right person to drive and improvise. And as the business grows, It is vital for the system to work without co-founders, with handful of hired new middle-line leaders.

Rima Paul finally became the 13th hire of the LAM with Employee ID: **LM-13-013**. A cool alliteration formed with "13".

LM: Legal (Alphabets) Matrix

13: The year of hire (2013),

013: 13th Member [Yes, less than 999 hiring in a year]

* * * * * *

Rima is quite energetic & compassionate in her communication and the approach towards dealing with people. She was a leader, with more on the listening side that allows enough space and time to tell your story. A perfect HR to whom everyone can share the concerns without keeping layers. At the same time, the job too seemed to be a perfect match that she expected from life, but hardly had any idea what was awaiting her.

There was a huge pile of activity work and hiring of more key roles in the Org, and Rima was all ready. But Jim's being very selective on the right fit, made her work more challenging. Her dedication during and off the office hours was impressive. It was a six days job, with Saturday pushed to be half-day after Rima joined, to facilitate work-life balance for the employees. However, for co-founders like Jim, work-life balance is just a fancy word, as both words "work" and "life" are one or the same, work is life & life is work… until both are married.

LAM has horsepower

LAM was expanding its arms and wings covering multiple locations across India. The team size increased to forty-four now.

Rima and Jim became the concrete base of the organization with Rima handling HR & Admin and Jim handling operations, business, data and designing. The other stuff such as recruitment plans, various investment discussions, sales pitch for new clients, approaching potential investors in the market & many more were either handled by Chadha sir or the trio team (Jim, Chadha, Rima). They worked vigorously to take LAM to new heights.

Jim's passion and Rima's sincere dedication brought them closer to one cause "Organization's Success". They got so indulged in their work that many times Chadha sir had to remind Rima that "Lady, it is late 9 o'clock, go home".

They both evidently marked their presence in accelerating LAM in many aspects. Chadha sir also realized that he made the right decision by pulling Jim and then Rima in the organization; it was an Avengers team formation.

Recently, LAM has on-boarded 2 high paying front-end partners to leverage the power of LAM and get the volume of requirements. Everyone looks joyful at the workplace being part of a fast-growing company.

LAM also promotes feel good factors

*There were surprise appreciation **pat**, recognitions, hike rewards, team outings, and promotion announcements for the employees to encourage inter department communications for sharing thoughts, ideas and fun, it helps the team stay connected & motivated.*

Love is coincidence

In the race of LAM's growth story, Jim & Rima tend to spend most of the time together, getting to know each other more. They don't just discuss data, PPT, issues, & solutions but also their likes – dislikes, interest – disinterest, and enjoy each other's company. They are seen together on lunch, tea breaks, sharing their food, ideas & thoughts. And these made both of them to incline towards each other. Yes, Jim finally mentioned that "13" is Jim's lucky number.

Apart from being a sincere employee, Rima was also a great cook. The amazing fish curry along with rice & vegetable salad, and the mouth melting Cheesy Maggi, were the two secrets from her treasure box, which her colleagues often enjoyed. Now their togetherness was not just seen within the office boundaries but outside the office too. They regularly caught up on Sundays, went for a movie, lunch or shopping together; and found reasons to do so.

Presentation Day

With time, the attraction between Jim and Rima developed to such an extent that there was not a single day that they would miss wishing good day to each other before starting the day. The passion towards work and attraction towards each other kept both of them energetic and punctual at office.

One very day, Rima came to the office in an adorable saree as she had to present an on-going recruitment to higher executives. As she walked in the office, Jim was perplexed to see her in a saree (Saree is a garment consisting of a long piece of cotton or silk wrapped around the body with one end draped over one shoulder). Both shared good wishes to each other and moved on to their work without much talking, as Rima was in a hurry to get her presentation ready.

She was looking even more confident with her attitude and the dressing sense. Her face was wearing some kind of natural glow that day, or maybe make-up not sure.

The presentation was going to start in an hour, she checked the arrangements beforehand to have a seamless and uninterrupted presentation. As Rima planned, everything started perfectly and on time. Rima was addressing Finance, Retail executives and the CEO. While the meeting proceeded, Jim noticed Rima's Saturday was longer than Sunday. I know hearing this might have brought many lascivious thoughts in your mind. But let me explain to you "Saturday is Petticoat (a type of skirt worn under a saree) and Sunday is Saree here". So I meant, her petticoat was visible near the bottom from one side & looked weird, especially for a perfectionist like Rima.

Being her well-wisher Jim was disturbed & not able to resist. He had 2 choices – either as a to-be-lover, he would ask her to stop the meeting and get her Saturday and Sunday right, or as a CEO he would focus on her presentation rather than dress and do not let others notice what crossed his eyes. It was a tough call to be made, and immediately.

Mr Chadha, who was sitting diagonally opposite to Jim, noticed Jim's face and realized that there was something unusual in the room. Jim's eyes fell back on Chadha and a stream of blood ran through his whole body; "What's wrong", "how to control?"

And immediately, Jim pushed his chair slightly to take the glass of water kept on the table, and in the 100th fraction of a second, he trembled his hand and water fell on a few leaders attending the meeting. The situation became awkward, Jim immediately said sorry and asked for an apology. Everyone in the room got distracted and the meeting had to get postponed for a while. Jim created a third option spontaneously and executed it well with a perfect balance.

Mr. Chadha, though unconscious about Rima's wardrobe malfunction, but got the vibes of Jim's intention. A powerful human brain has the ability to sense, which is untapped by most of us.

The meeting resumed with Rima and other executives back from the restroom, and went fluent uninterrupted this time. :)

Next day morning, everyone looked fresh & started the day as usual. After the morning stand up, Chadha sir asked Jim to stay inside for a minute, while the rest of them were asked to move. Chadha sir had to intimate Jim on a serious note but diplomatically; he asserted "When we encourage gender diversity at work, we must empower every woman employee and make their presence our strength rather than a hindrance to our business. Rest you are smart enough, I just suggest you to be cautious.". Boomm! This signal astounds Jim. Deep.

Jim was somehow trying to limit his interactions with Rima but now it was not easy to stay away from her, and the same was the story on Rima's side. Things got settled over time and a few more stories added in their list.

Several weeks passed, knowingly or unknowingly they got so addicted to each other that the impact can be seen on their work now. Jim was unable to pay the same focus or deliver the quality that was seen before in his work, since his mind and energy both are distracted.

Birthday surprise

It was 10th August around 9 in the morning, being Sunday Rima was still lying on her bed with her dreams. The phone rings and she has to open her eyes & look out of the blanket. She answered the phone with half-opened eyes. A loving & magical voice saying "Good morning! The sleeping beauty!"

came up. It was none other, but Jim, "Hey Good morning.. Jim!. You got up so early on Sunday", Rima replied.

Jim, very quickly, "Achha (Ok) Listen I am going for a gathering today with my ex-colleagues at Fun city near GT Park and you are coming too".

Before even Rima could utter anything, Jim said (softly) "Please don't say No… Pleasssseeee", Jim pleaded.

Rima: Hmmm Ok, nodded her head, and both planned to meet at 4 outside GT Park.

Jim reached before Rima could arrive (as usual girls take their own sweet time to prepare herself). Jim was sitting on a bench a bit inside the park, could sense that Rima had arrived and looked outside as his phone rings.

Rima, appeared in a black calf-length dress with a gold color shrug, giving a perfect match to her beauty, which was enough to increase Jim's heartbeat, in a rhythm of a moving steam train. Yes, Jim is mad for Rima and couldn't help noticing every single dress of Rima, a true lover, or maybe, it was Rima's dress selection that perfectly suits her persona.

Both shared the greetings, then Rima asked "where are your friends?"

Jim: "One canceled as she got some unplanned guests at home and another due to personal emergency. It's only both of us now."

"Oh is it.?" Rima replied with a little hesitation but trying not to spoil his mood and the moment so they carry on with their walk. During the walk, Jim revealed (with an innocent smile) that he is planning for a 6pm movie and she should not say No, as "It is his Birthday today.." Rima looks at him surprisingly with a mix of expressions, both love & sweet anger at the same time. "Got you man! You are telling the truth now"…and couldn't resist from her sweet smile in return, which was enough to give a green signal to him and energize his rest of the day.

Both started moving towards the theatre, the lovely breeze and chirping birds were turning the evening pleasant for a walk. After the movie they enjoyed a lovely dinner at a nearby Rajdhani Junction – the place was looking perfect with soothing lights & music for cherishing each other's presence. They were so indulged in that moment that they kept on talking & walking till late night. Looks like the naughty lie with acceptance, romantic evening, & the lovely dinner did some magic on them.

"Memories are created when two people are in a moment with 100% honesty and trust upon each other, especially if there is a physical touch*. Life becomes worth living in the moment and acts as an invaluable source of energy for the days when you feel lonely."

It was around 11:30 that they made a final move to their places, with a hug & pluck of kiss on Rima's palm, like a lover's (hesitant) first kiss.

After returning home, Rima received a msg saying "Thanks for making your presence on my special day, this was the best birthday I could ever have. From J". Again their chatting continued till late night.

Next day morning, Rima managed to reach the office timely, however Jim did not appear.

Jim ruined investor's catchup

On the other hand, Chadha sir got a sudden plan to meet a few investors; while Jim is in perception that Chadha sir will manage the meetings well & he will mark his presence over call, if needed.

The day passed but Jim didn't turn up as he was still lying on his bed wrapped with last evening memories & cherishing them. By the evening, Chadha sir called Jim asking for some supporting data to present the investors for the final discussion. Jim made

---

* *Our body cells have brain and memory-storage of its own, that's the reason you can know if someone familiar touches you and the reason that in many communities, people join their own hands for greetings as they don't want the unwanted memories in their life.*

it ready at the last minute & shared it directly with investors, didn't have any idea what was going to happen tomorrow.

He had to look at all the facts consciously and make the pitch absolutely appealing. Since Chadha sir didn't want any scope to misdrive it. As usual, he trusted his work so didn't pay much attention to the last-minute preparation.

The next day when the discussion was carried out, everyone realized that shared numbers & the pointers were not appropriate, which did not sound appealing to investors for sure. The meetings ended with some signs of disappointment on their face. Investors left with a note that they will get back and mentioned "LAM needs some more work improvement and focus on data accuracy".

Everyone left the room without talking to each other.

This was big enough for Jim to open his eyes and turn him awake. 'Such negligence at these levels can't be afforded and can make them pay huge.' The consciousness that he should have paid to the work was compromised and may cause a hit to all as an Organisation or a team.

That night after going back home, his inner soul & spirit continued to haunt him. Many thoughts were flying around his mind & brain. "The objective for leaving a MNC & joining the startup was not to have a relaxed job while indulged into a bonus, a Love life, etc"

Next day morning before Chadha sir could express anything, Jim takes the courage to stand in front of him, bending the head down, face turned red, confesses, "I realize from yesterdays and the previous lessons that the path I was moving may hit me hard, not only me it may affect everyone else at work directly. I can handle the emotions better and decide the priorities. I request for a week-time, you will see a better version of mine soon."

Chadha sir couldn't believe the realization that Jim came through, he couldn't control his sentiments too, "I see great confidence in you, your abilities and your passion, and am sure this will not let us go down. *Self Realization is the first step towards success."* He replied. "Carry on, the team is waiting for the standup and Rima too (with teasing tone)"

Reincarnation – A Choice or a decision

Now he has two choices towards resurrection. Either focus 100% on career and let the love life go; or to give the career growth a priority without losing his love life, by making a temporary distance with Rima. For the next few hours, he kept on figuring out the ways on how to sort it out together, before it gets too late.

Very next day after the lunch break, he takes the courage to put the same choice to her.

"Rima, I strongly believe that whatever roles we are in, we must not let our personal matter impact the businesses. Right or wrong?". "Absolutely", Rima replied.

"I don't want to be diplomatic here since this is the most serious matter of our lives and so putting my thoughts straight away. In these nearly 1 year, I have truly enjoyed your company and cherished all the time spent with you. Your presence made me feel complete and more contentful. I hope you felt the same.

I can't forecast my future and I don't want to since I love my present. Would love to give this present a future."

"Considering everyone's betterment, I want to give ourself a break here with a commitment that 2 years later we will come back to hold each other's hand and to make two soul as one… During these 2 years, we will ensure our focus only on LAM and our individual growth. This is what my thoughts are. I understand you may have different views which is totally fine, I would respect it.", Jim continued with intensity, with Rima being patient listener.

"Or, else we should move individually towards our own path and for that, I may have to put you on another vertical basis of your interest.". "Rima!"

Rima was speechless by hearing these heavy words. Her eyes were widely opened staring at the opposite wall, not understanding 'How to react & What to react'?

Her heart was beating faster as if she was going to miss a train… a train which took her through this adventurous journey in the last few months, encouraging & accompanying her on her path. She was lonely, clueless, and looking for some guidance, He has shown utmost care for her, and how could they depart easily. She has to fight back. All these were going in her mind, while Jim gave all space and time.

Rima looked anxious & confused, before she could express herself, Jim holding her hand, said "It's not easy to decide all this in a minute. Go home, relax, talk to your heart & soul, and your parents too. Take some time, think freely & wisely and let me know, I will be happy with your decision whatever it may be."

Later after giving a deep thought, Rima replies "I am yours. And will be yours. Let's make a success story of LAM."

It is totally okay for a leader to live a Love-life being at work, however a true entrepreneur can't have both the pie at the same time; to achieve success. Therefore, one may need to take the toughest calls. An entrepreneur must learn to balance both "Love" & "Career" without distracting the focus on Goal, and take the tough call if needed.

A comeback as Warriors

Jim Kaushal has made a strong comeback without a pinch of regret, and actually no point of regret. Rather he is much stronger, to focus on making the best version of him. Listing down all his goals and bucketing them as short term & long term goals. Big goals were broken into daily goals and then like a ruthless warrior, hitting all the problems right at bullseye. This reminds him of the way he killed all opponents in a 10/10 shot with the bullpup (gun), when he played "counter strike (CS) – condition zero" at college. The sound "puff puff" with every bullet hitting the enemy. Aaahh! What a game!

|| Recap ||

Best Takeaway Tips on Business Establishment

PRINCIPLE #1
Plan & Act for all the Eight Departments (Be it just system, no human employee).
Conscious Action.

PRINCIPLE #2
Do NOT miss the meeting of Management and R&D Dept, for taking leap of success.

PRINCIPLE #3
A Robust communication system – Metrics, Dashboard, Track(MDT).

PRINCIPLE #4
Independent Validation(Quality) Team with right mind, gutt & environment.

PRINCIPLE #5
Identify & Pay Sufficient to the Leaders.

PRINCIPLE #6
There is always an option, a Comeback. Today!

PRINCIPLE #7
It's not about how much you know, It is about how much you implement.

PART FIVE

THE FRAMEWORK TO SUCCESS

Journey of Reaching His Destiny

"The only constant in life is **change**" – by Heraclitus, a Greek philosopher

Indian economy has gone through many cycles, since independence from British rule. But one thing remained **constant** throughout the economic progress across decades: *the dominance of family-owned businesses in India*. **Birla family** is one of them.

This large empire was started by small cotton trader 'Shiv Narayan Birla' in the 1860s. Baldeo Das and sons were active supporters of many national movements, including the Banaras Hindu University founded by Pt. Madan Mohan Malaviya. They built **Laxminarayan Temple** in Delhi and all Hindus, including harijans were welcomed in this temple. **Aditya Birla Group** is among the largest manufacturers of Black Carbon and Aluminium, and has presence in 35 countries; and employs large workforce that is much higher than many MNCs in the world.

(From left) Aditya Birla, Kumar Mangalam Birla, G.D. Birla and B.K. Birla…

*Credit: Livemint.com

The Group is also well known for establishing many prestigious colleges (BIT Mesra, BITS Pilani, etc), research centers, hospitals, mutual funds.

Do you know, Birla family owns the **world's second largest mobile networ**k (Vodafone Idea), Hindalco, Hindustan Times (1924), Hindustan Motors (Manufacturer of Ambassador). Awesome, isn't it?

Once Jim was fortunate to attend a great workshop at Bangalore (India); the city well known for lovely weather and IT Professionals. The one takeaway that mutated him is, "Thinking has become a disease*. And since everyone is having the same disease, it looks normal."

"Our mind is an instrument that should be relaxed, once used for a task. Not only people keep thinking repetitive and useless, but they also tend to think harmful.

Let's perceive the other way, As we grow from a newborn to a young; we learn to control the movement of hands, legs, and other parts of our body system, but what about the mind; shouldn't that too be a part of the same growing and controlling system?"

Jim was able to connect with the reason why, 'It is called that morning meditation and chanting of Gayatri mantra (or any such mantra) was so powerful', it helped him to use his tool, called mind, more focused and effective. And so, his parents and many others are doing prayers, without being aware of the actual science behind it.

The 6-step Success Manifesto

Once, Jim was on a call with his Delhi-based cousin, a CA-turned-businessman, about operations, management, and vision mapping. He couldn't help noticing, the need for a framework that can be referred to in the journey for success.

---

* Dis-ease (Disease) happens when things get out of balance. For example, there is nothing wrong with cells multplying in the body, but when this process continues in disregard of the total organism, we have disease.

Jim has been experiencing it, and it was the time to give it a shape. He kept talking and sketching a step-by-step framework that he was implementing unconsciously in all his execution and making it a success.

This framework has 6-steps, three steps for inward exercise, and the other three steps for outward implementation.

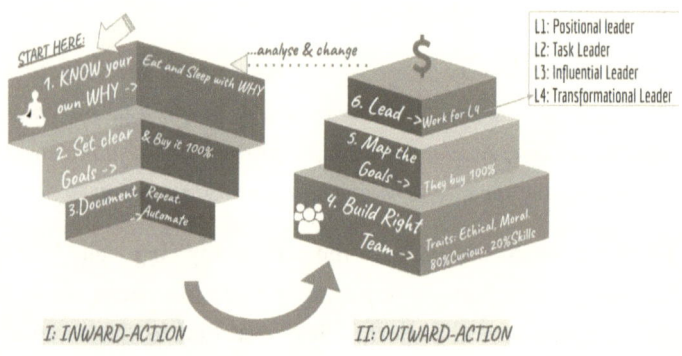

Image: *6-step success manifesto*

Inward-Actions

Inward-Action, Step#1: Why

Know your own why. Ask a series of questions to yourself and mentor. Go through fishbone, Pareto or simply 5-Why technique (These are world's most renowned techniques to solve the problems). More clear the Why is, impactful and Simpler the Rest of Stages are. Spend at least 2days on this step with focus.

Inward-Action, Step#2: Set M.R.T. Goals

Set clear goals, and more importantly, "buy-it 100%". Goals should have 3 ingredients: Measurable, Realistic and tagged with Turnaround time (TAT), in short Goals must be **MRT.**

M: Measurable

Measurable goals and objectives are essential for evaluating progress in any situation, be it work, learning, or personal development.

R: Realistic

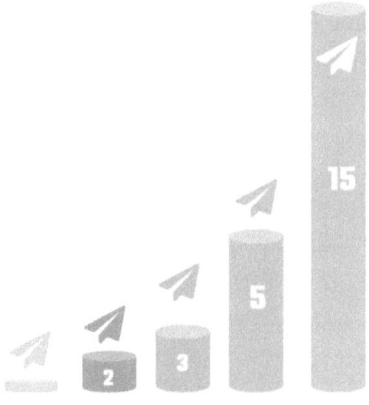

Image: *Progressive realistic, attainable and measurable goals*

Unrealistic goals are more likely to discourage you through the process and you will be likely to give up on the goal. Setting realistic and progressive attainable goals will retain motivation and stickiness to timelines, culminating in the successful completion of a goal.

T: Turnaround time

Image: *A timer or deadline is important part of goal*

Turnaround time (TAT) is the time interval from the time of submission of a process to the time of the completion of the process, or simply time to attain the goal. DEADLINES are very important.

This goal as the writing part would take 80% of total time. While just 20% of time goes for "buying it from the heart", it will contribute to 80% of goal success. 20% of quality time will control the 80% of outcome. [Credit: Pareto principle]

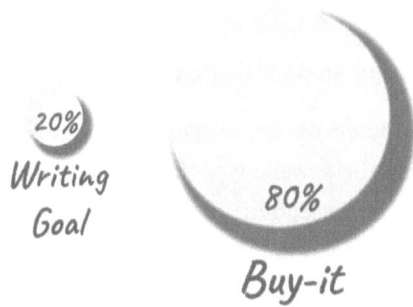

Image: *Contribution of writing and buying-it from heart*

Inward-Action, Step#3: Document and Automate

The vision & goals in mind are not enough if cannot be shared and well-conceived by the team. Document the goals and path to achieve. Travel the path to goals yourself, or dry run as relevant. Repeat this journey. With time, plug-in a system to minimize manual intervention.

Simply speaking, A Vision contains many Goals and the Goals have to go through repeated actions.

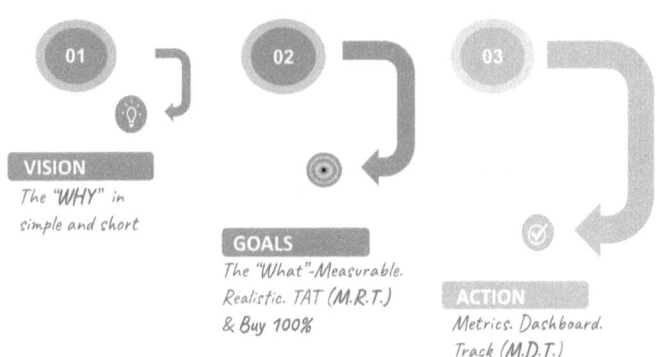

Image: *One view on a vision to Goals to Actions*

Outward-Actions

Outward-Action, Step#4: Build the Right Team

Build a team based on ethics, curiosity, and passion. Know your team-members well, especially before hiring. Analyze their mindset and capability in different circumstances like over a walk, a coffee, or an unknown instance.

Outward-Action, Step#5: Team Goals

Map organization goals with their goals. Yes, they should also buy it 100%.

Outward-Action, Step#6: Lead Like a Leader

Setting goals and expecting things to happen on itself, won't work. Become a leader; and one should learn to become a "transformational leader", to make the magic happen.

It's proven that inspiration for technology breakthroughs are **not rooted** in technological knowledge alone. The learning and expertise of other knowledge areas such as Maths, Science, Psychology. Technology is necessary, critical necessary – but they are **not sufficient**. To have that magic, the 6-Step success manifesto must be considered for building the inward-outward connection.

"An organization's ability to learn, and translate that learning into action rapidly, is the ultimate competitive advantage. -Jack Welch, Former CEO of General Electric"

Why Goals are Important

Most of us today don't have goals in our life. Having no Goal leads to wastage of huge energy and time, as one

Journey of Reaching His Destiny | **143**

travels aimlessly in different directions; and hence they don't succeed.

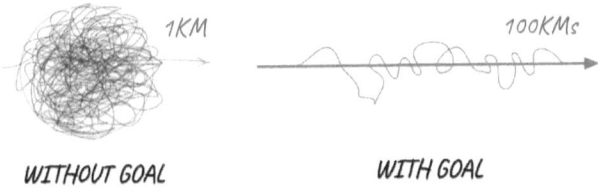

WITHOUT GOAL *WITH GOAL*

Image: *Journey without goal and with goal*

The goal of human beings is like a destination for a Train. Imagine, there is no captain inside the Train; what will happen?

"It will have a 0% probability to reach the destination; forget destination, a high-chance that it lands in a deserted endpoint, or meets an accident."

Having goals and working on it, also uncaps the abundance of "potential of our mind". The more you think about, the more you attract similar energies to help you.

There are four Fundamental Techniques that Jim constantly used to remain focused:

1. Staying 'Lean'

    Japanese methodology towards the removal of waste. Anything that is not helpful in the path of Goal is waste.

2. Playing the favorite game of 'Snake and Ladder'

    Snake and Ladder is an ancient Indian board game for two or more players regarded as a worldwide classic.

Let's modify the objects. Plan your "**essentials**", say book, motivational videos, quotes, healthy snacks, are to be kept closer and reachable, imagining them as "Ladder"; and non-essentials like Social media apps, Junk foods, negative people are to be kept at a distance or extra steps to reach, imagining them as "Snake".

More the ladders you step, faster to goals you move.

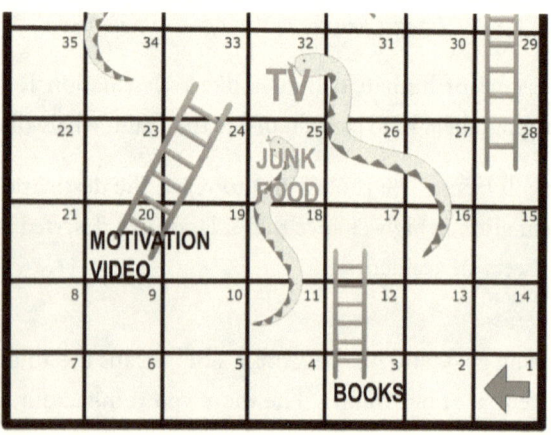

3. Learn to Say 'No', gracefully

   Less-successful people say 'Yes' for almost everything; while successful people say 'No' for everything which is not a part of their goal.

   Here are a few phrases that would be helpful to say 'No' in tough situations:

   – Shall I get back later, need some time?

   – I am little occupied, let me check my calendar

   – I can recommend someone more suitable

4. Not to get into 'Sunk Cost' Fallacy Even the smartest people fall in this category and end up with a double loss.

    - Bought your favorite food for INR 500, you continue to eat even after your stomach goes upset, due to the price it involves.
    - Found that movie is totally boring, still end up watching it; since you paid for it.
    - Bought certain stocks in trading, going in Loss. Just because you have invested before, you keep investing. Similar case by startup Investors.

        The solution is to 'Acknowledge' that you have failed or something has lost, and put an 'End (full-stop)'.

Setup the culture for Inner Engineering

"At recurring intervals, our routine turns monotonous. And many times it impacts the outcome directly. Yes or No?". Jim knew this well from his first Job.

Hence, it was very important for Jim to work upon the self-motivation aspect of employees, apart from the daily task and career development. "Strengthening of willpower is important to weaken the procrastination tendencies."

Various self-affirmations were prepared as cards and made mandatory to be read out (randomly) by picking the cards. A new ritual being talked and taken into action as a 45days challenge. It invited an extensive discussion among several core members but meant to be executed with no choice. Unconsciousness & Self-belief had to be programmed by Jim.

Few Powerful Affirmations being used at LAM Technologies:

"Every thought I have, it helps me to create my desired life"

"I am easy and relaxed. Nothing worries me"

"I am cheerful in every situation, content and smiling"

"I clear my toxic emotions that hurts me, routinely by talking to someone relevant, or writing it down"

"Social media & Internet is just a platform that helps me learn,
and spread positive vibrations".

"Social media doesn't distract-away me from my daily goals, I watch only relevant content & positive messages."

"I am the master of my fate:
I am the captain of my soul."

"I use filtered words that energize me,
That creates optimism and positive vibrations"

"DON'T DREAM OF IT, ***TRAIN*** *FOR IT."*

A well-executed morning to win 80% of the day

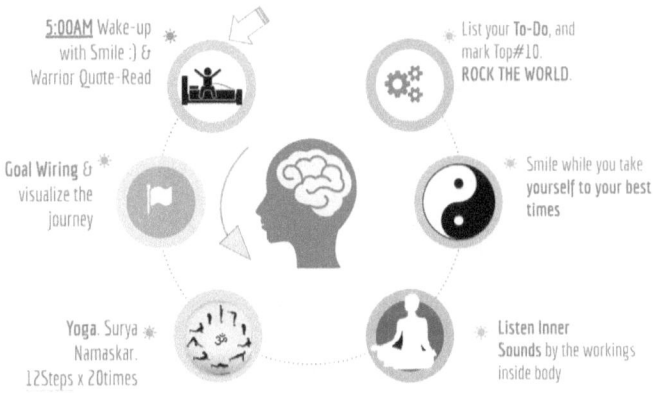

1. **Wake-up early with Smile**. Read a motivational Warrior Quote. Quote example "Let's accomplish what others are afraid of"

2. **Goal Repetition**: Read the Goal. And then imagine completion.

3. **Yoga**: A healthy body caves a healthy mind and brain. Surya Namaskar 20 times.

4. **Mediate inward**: A calm mind to improve focus, and channelize/reduce those 60,000 thoughts that come daily.

5. **Mediate outward**: Resonate with your worldly dream & understand the complementary forces of nature.

6. **Check the checklist**: Time to kick-off. List down your task of the day by writing on paper. Checklist is the most powerful tool in the world, even more

than Spreadsheet. Jim realized and smiled. Tasks categorized into 3-types of checkbox(s)

1. Blank: Task not started
2. Dot: Task is in Progress
3. Tick-mark: Task completed

☐ Not started
⊙ inProgress
✓ Completed

Image: *Checklist management: Not started, inProgress, Completed*

*Implement the 4H Rule: When you find something good, ensure to mention the Happy part in 4 lines/words at least, and when something goes wrong, do not repeat. Am sure this is the reverse with most people. A infographic to add on 4H.

Growth has two directions – horizontal and vertical

The variety of services at LAM technologies was increasing exponentially, along with a replication of the business framework to new cities. The company bagged 250+ services with its presence in 50 cities across India. Jim also hired a business head to expand in other countries. None of the legal agents, property dealers, CAs, Local courts, Notaries were left untouched. New customer segments were being targeted with awareness about the need for legality, through various channels of marketing – Affiliate, ATL, BTL, Door-to-door workforce, Social Media.

This was no more an innovation, but a **disruption** that the world was talking about.

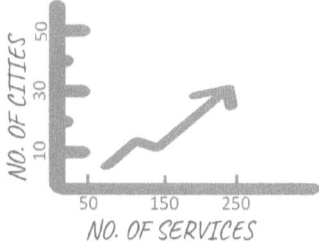

Image: *Growth curve of LAM*

As a leader, you need philosophies constantly pumping into the heart of your team, and worth to mention, even if implemented it takes time to produce the outcome. LAM was growing bigger and bigger, not because of what was being conveyed or implementing disciplinary rules, but what was actually happening behind the closed doors, at the heartland of LAM employees. People were regularly found promoting & recognizing each other's work. There was no "Me" but "We", "One LAM". A **trust** was established among all, the most powerful ingredient.

The straight-forward example on the leader-versus-rules theory shared by Chadha sir – "Apple (Company) and Steve Jobs"

1. *Apple pushes out Steve Jobs*

2. *Apple goes bankrupt*

3. *Apple pulls back Steve Jobs*

4. *Apple goes immensely profitable*

There were rules and protocols even after Steve Jobs was out, but without the right ingredient, the right motivation, the company was almost shut. And then goes highly profitable once Steve Jobs is back.

All the meeting rooms at LAM were having posters with great philosophies, hand-picked by both co-founders, and rooms were named after successful people of the world – Elon Musk, Bill Gates, Dr. APJ Abdul Kalam, Mother Teresa.

Superman's secret revealed

Jim was spending hours visualizing the progressive path of LAM (Legal Alphabets Matrix), ensuring all alphabets of Legal services be embraced in his style. He used to walk alone with his deep internal thoughts – What are the new services that can be added; How to improve – People, Revenue & Process; Is there a new segment to leverage in current capacity; What's new today for the organization & team?; and many more.

These thoughts were the food for the progressive journey of LAM. Hence, to summarize the overall activity of Jim into two parts: staying lonely but focused, and then multi-tasking across departments like Superman's ability.

These were the secrets that only Jim knew. Secret that even multi-tasking was one task at a time, being done at a faster pace. Then he recalled his engineering classes – "Multitasking is a logical extension in which CPU switches jobs so frequently that users can interact with each job while it is running and creating interactive computing". (Credit – Operating system concepts by Silberschatz-Peterson-Galvin).

Some fellow-colleagues commented, "Jim you have Bolt-speed in closing a task. What keeps your mind & body instrumental and in harmony?"

* * * * * *

Kaizen is one of the most decorated Japanese terms; and the simplest definition boils down to "Continuous improvement".

Immense hard work with actions breaks all the barriers and sets new records.

Kaizen along with immense hard work led to actions after actions, goals after goals, and accomplishing almost all set milestones. And once the team is about to accomplish a vision they brainstormed, there is an update and movement to the creation of a new vision. Jim's note on connecting actions, goals and vision are

1. Actions using MDT (Metrics, Dashboard, Track) framework

2. Goals using MRT (Measurable, Realistic, TAT) framework

3. Improvise Vision (When vision is about to accomplish)

*Both MDT and MRT Frameworks are discussed early in the book.

Image: *Actions to goals to vision*

It was just marvelous to experience the continuous improvement, one above the other. This is nothing but a compound effect.

The Compound effect had enormous enormous power. The twice usage of "enormous" is for a reason. This 'Compound effect' terminology is amazing. *Bring a small change constantly, each time on top of what is achieved, and you will see an unbelievable large impact.*

Let's mathematically prove:

- 1.01 => Improvement by 0.1 unit
- 0.99 => Downgrade by 0.1 unit

A little extra push consistently, 1.01, multiplied 365 times is 37.8; and when 0.99 is multiplied by itself for 365 times, attains to 0.03.

$$1.01^{365} = 37.8$$

$$0.99^{365} = 0.03$$

37.8 vs 0.03, there is a monumental difference and if you can put this same approach for 3years, this would end up taking you 54000 times ahead. Unimaginable. Agree?

Take control. Give control

With the system automated one after another, new people taking leadership positions, Jim was no more a common executioner, but a very precise one. Jim has to be very precise from an organization's point of view too; his one hour cost was the summation of the salary of one or more of his staff. Jim has to shade his skin of many colors, and work very specific as per a predefined plan.

Success was no more a destination or some $10 million in his bank account; Success was clearly about **progressively achieving the goals** he set for himself.

(To add content about Why creating Leaders in Middle line)

LAM is doing wonders and touching the soaring heights, unimagined. With more leaders onboarding, Jim was getting some peace of mind. Juniors from the same college used to approach for tips and guidance, which he was embracing. He also launched a platform where sincere startup enthusiasts used to catch up once a fortnight at his new bigger LAM Office.

The whole ambience of a bigger office with Jim's character was influencing everyone.

* * * * * *

With growing numbers in the bank account, it was the time to get set the long-pending Financial planning, which ideally should be from the day1 you earn. Anyway, after making some decent experiments & knowledge download, **Financial Intelligence** was the new buzz among his session. It says "Every professional must have this 6-Jars of Financial Planning", he learned from an astounding workshop.

Credit: Secrets of the millionaire mind, By T. Harv Eker

1. Financial Freedom Account (FFA): The golden goose account, used for passive income. Never ever spend this money.

2. Necessity Account (NEC): Towards managing your everyday expenses and bills.

3. Education (EDU): To spend on continuous learning

4. Long term Savings for spend (LTSS): This is the account for bigger expenses, say family vacation, bigger home, car

5. PLAY: To spend every month on purchase or spend you don't usually do.

6. GIVE: Giving away without expectations. A sign of abundance, and attracts the same.

Now it was the time to set discipline towards achieving financial freedom along with helping beginners who want to start the entrepreneurial journey, and financial-needy by giving out some part of earning without any expectation.

* * * * *

Jim revised his definition of Success as "To help billions live happily doing what they love". The next version of Jim Kaushal has begun.

He is an icon for startups, addressing the crowd to solve real-time challenges in the 'passion vs profit' battleground. He speaks on how to prepare youth communities to opt for the right path, to dream what they love, to create their own success stories, and to overcome failures; truly based on his real-life experiences.

The Go-getter is not just an executioner, he walks like a storm stimulating many thoughts and transforming aspirants. Nonetheless, he is also leaving his footprints everywhere whichever department or the projects he is working with.

The knowledge and experiences he has been traveling so far, must give a ladder for the coming generations to reach their milestones. And so he added a new goal of writing a book – a book is the best way to broadcast your thoughts, your wisdom. This way, Jim can help millions of employees & leaders towards creating powerful systems and tap their potential. He is shuttling like an active influencer across social media, blogs, articles, one-on-one, and everywhere.

The blogs & articles on practical challenges, materials on how to start a business & grow consistently; all are getting penned to be available for the enthusiasts & next generation.

He started getting invites from groups and societies to share his invaluable inputs. And with time, he is also called by big organizations, colleges to conduct events on how to opt for a path that has an amalgamation of passion, admiration, and wealth.

And this continues…

* * * * * *

The Man for the Moon

Almost two years later…

A calendar was blocked for a meeting with his new business partner Mrs. Murthy. Mrs Murthy was running a Law firm, with a presence in 45 cities across the world. She had heard a lot about Jim and his captivating personality from many, including Mr Chadha; and finally both were going to meet towards a bigger vision.

Jim was well settled in his favorite black-suit, white tee, and blue denim jeans. Mrs. Murthy reaches LAM corporate office.

Both shared greetings, and looked excited to discuss their proposal of taking LAM in all the states – to bring all the legal services online in all the regions at the customer's fingertips.

They had three meetings in the six months of time. The first two catch ups were held at LAM and the third one was planned at a new convention room next to UB City, her preferred meeting spot. Jim reached the venue 10 mins before and made his stuff ready for presentation. Mrs. Murthy is yet to appear. And soon he gets a message saying she would be joining him a little late and apologized as she got stuck in an unexpected call. While he was waiting, he got to interact with other executives from her organization. Finally, the meeting got started, with a big apology from Mrs. Murthy for reaching late. The overwhelming meeting went for 2 hrs 15 mins.

After the meeting got over, she couldn't resist herself from sharing her challenge.

Jim was patient during the whole conversation, and got to know that other than this Law firm she is heading an event management firm as well; where they connect the renowned speakers, authors, life coaches with the right set of audiences through events & workshops in various cities.

She is disturbed due to one of the events scheduled 2-days later at Coimbatore (Tamil Nadu, India) for 5000 audiences. The Speaker who was the Man for that event has asked to postpone it, due to some personal constraints. Such an episode in event management not only causes downgrading the brand but also big financial loss. Now, Mrs. Murthy has two choices – either postpone the event or find a replacement who can take over the event at brief notice. He should also have a presentable attitude and remarkable confidence to speak before a big intellectual crowd.

You have to develop your skillset & strengthen your true potential in such a way that you don't need to run behind success, but success will come to your door. //

He has developed his skillset & strengthened himself in such a way that he doesn't need to run behind success, i.e. success was coming to his door. His skillset and personality made him stand on the other side of the audience.

On the continuation, she expressed her thoughts saying, "Mr. Kaushal, You come with vast experience in starting a business from scratch, building the team, went through failures, stood up, and made your way to several milestones."

"I may not be surprised if it sounds interesting and a great opportunity to you. I truly believe that we may not get someone better than you to engage my audience."

Jim's heartbeat was running at almost double pace. He was thrilled to hear.

She also mentioned that – don't let any fear overcome you, it is human nature to think like a river and get carried away in our own created thoughts. I have seen many first time speakers how they start with no background and how they end up being celebrated & lavishly paid.

Jim is in deep thought…

"Okay let's say if, you are asked to address thousands of school kids on Alphabets, phonemics and the Numbers. Would you hesitate, No right?"

"Because we were masters at this."

"Similarly, you are well-versed & thorough by startup journey & various ups & down; you can easily present to millions.. Rest you have a great attracting personality.

"What is 2 multiplied 22? "

Jim within fraction of seconds – "44".

"A to Z with correct phonics"

"A for Aluminium, B for Basket…"

She signalled to halt. "Would you hesitate answering the same before millions or billions of people? Will there be any fear?"

Jim perceived. And then Mrs. Murthy mentioned something that Jim cherished forever; another golden nugget of life –

F.E.A.R. has two choices –

(1) Forget Everything And Run-away OR

(2) Face Everything And Rise.

Difference is attitude. The choice is yours.

And coincidentally Jim got to see the famous quote recently pasted on LAM wall, "I knew that if I failed I wouldn't regret that, but I knew one thing I might regret is not trying.~Jeff Bezos".

…and we all know what is coming next.

Life is a summation of your own thoughts

With his new path towards helping millions of others to live more meaningful; life was full of opportunity & excitement. New people & new learnings were getting added to his list. He takes the joy of reading 3-books a month and exploring various techniques to inspire others. As it is said "A book can be your best friend; which can be a source of energy when no one is around. A book can enlighten and lead you in the right direction, it develops your mind and gives knowledge & lessons of life which can be admired for a lifetime."

The next version of Jim as an Author, as a Coach has arisen. He is moving ahead in the world of authorship, exchanging thoughts with the world's topmost Leaders, Authors and Life coach. The quality of a leader and an entrepreneur reflects from his every statement and actions.

His Potential, Passion & Never give up attitude made him stand incredibly before success, made him stand on the other side of the stage. He is no more a consumer, but a creator.

Jim has become one of the most eminent motivational speakers in the world. He is traveling across the geographies being a channel of knowledge towards dreams and passion. And helped many lives turning their **Passion into Profit** & **Dreams into Profession**.

"Doubt kills more dreams than failure – Suzy Kassem"

***Image:** Jim taking path where his real interest and work was same*

* * * * *

"It never gets easier. You just get stronger."

While moving ahead in life, we may have to let a few things go; maybe some habit, or some people. Sometimes, due to lack of time, or difference in frequency. One of his best friends who is crazy about Guns, used to talk about "Politics & Porn" and had to be overlooked. While there were friends & relatives demanding time – to meet them, to hear them, to solve silly problems. Jim let a few of them go. "May God give me the right strength and knowledge", Jim prayed.

Everyone who has intersected in your journey, be grateful for their presence and move forward.

> *"If there are people getting left behind while you move ahead in life.*
> *It also implies you are growing. All are not meant to stay until the end."*

"you are an average of 5 people, you spend the most time with."
Tips: Be it through online courses, workshops, videos. To move to page-header

All these experiences of losing people brought him disappointment a few times; but then with double energy, Jim assured to make a comeback on his **mission of Inspiring people**.

Overall, there is one thing that didn't change for Jim, was the definition of Success – "**Success is progressively achieving the goals that are set by oneself. Consciously.**" Jim by winning on himself every time, felt marvelous like a real-winner. He felt full of energy and sunshine of contentment that comes from within.

Epilogue

A Chatbot (Automated chating system) on Jim's Website, with 100s of potential client daily:

Bot: Hey there... Jim this side. care to chat?

Client: **Sure... why not.**

Bot: Awesome! I was wondering if you would like to create your goals & achieve it?

Client: **Yes! Sounds cool.**

Bot: Ok awesome! I'm sharing a link for this awesome course, which has changed life of millions and sure this would help you too.

Client: **Cool. I am in... Registered!**

Nice chatting with you

(LAM has turned into a world-class company as a prominent market-leader into legal Industry with 1000s of services, and renowned platform for service providers on the supply side; and corporates & common public on demand side. Jim continues

to have an ample Equity in LAM and is part of the board of Directors, along with worlds' top investors. Chadha sir and Mrs. Murthy are among the best friends who cheers and calls-out every success.

13th Employee Rima?

She is taking care of the household along with active participation in Jim's major discussions & his personal goals; happily married to Jim, happily accepted by Jim's mother, and a mother to two kids.

|| Recap ||

Theory for Reaching your Destiny

PRINCIPLE #1
Plan & Seed the right plants for Org.
Tap the abundance power of Unconsciousness.

PRINCIPLE #2
Keep Learning.
To-Self: Glass is half-empty; To-Others: Glass is half-full.

PRINCIPLE #3
Apply the 6-step Success Manifesto.

PRINCIPLE #4
Work on inner self. Meditate.
How you do one thing, is how you do Everything.

PRINCIPLE #5
Create Goals
Success is progressive achieving the goals that are pre-defined.

PRINCIPLE #6
Life is the Journey. Relax & Enjoy!

Images from Author's Diary

Banaras Hindu University, Varanasi

NITK Surathkal, Karnataka

Kite Fest at NITK Beach

Bucketkart

Your Leadership Playbook @ Amazon

Alok kumar

★★★★★ **Excellent Content, Loved it** 💚
Reviewed in India on 5 September 2020
Verified Purchase

Wao. Loved it. completed in just 30min. Very short and crisp. 100% would recommend it to all action takers. habit is our key... 💚💚

Shalin Mayank

★★★★★ **Awesome book for entrepreneur**
Reviewed in India on 4 October 2020
Verified Purchase

If you're an entrepreneur or are currently a wantrepreneur, this book will help you in so many ways. It will get you thinking in a different and important mindset.

sanjeev

★★★★★ **Superb content.**
Reviewed in India on 7 October 2020

Well written and beautifully handcrafted. A must handbook and pocket guide for all leaders. Looking for more publish from the author soon.

Image: *The Inspiring poem during childhood*
(In Hindi Language. Mother tongue of Author.)

रण बीच चौकड़ी भर-भर कर,
चेतक बन गया निराला था।
राणा प्रताप के घोड़े से,
पड़ गया हवा का पाला था।

गिरता न कभी चेतक तन पर,
राणा प्रताप का कोड़ा था।
वह दौड़ रहा अरि मस्तक पर,
यह आसमान का घोड़ा था।

जो तनिक हवा से बाग हिली,
लेकर सवार उड़ जाता था।
राणा की पुतली फिरी नहीं,
तब तक चेतक मुड़ जाता था।

Zero-to-Advance Package on Spreadsheet from Author

The Right Formula & Right Speed Decoded - 3Weeks Challenge

This 3-Phases online course gives you the secret for a strong foundation towards becoming an Expert in Google Sheets. The course is prepared with real-time experience from Industry and feedback from various experts, and includes detailed Tips, Video Materials, Assignments, Solved Problems and Online Test.

The 15 Proven Tools that every Analyst should Possess

These 15 Proven Tools along with complete scripts and formulas will support you and serve reference for your many upcoming tools. This may also serve towards getting your next Employee Award or Promotion, similar to many others. Includes the Automatic Certificate Generation and Printed, Invoice creation with your Current Geographic Location as Google Maps, and many more.

BONUS #1: 10x the Chance for Your Next Interview Call

When it comes to Interview Call, There is one thing that is 100% in your control - Your Resume. Two parts that form the resume are The **Right Keywords**, and **The Layout** that simplifies the appearance for the Interviewer. Top Resume Templates with latest Keywords and Contents of Business Analysts and Data Analysts.

BONUS #2: The 12-Mantras Book to Keep you Ahead

Narrating 12 greatest mantras from the author's personal journey of leading teams and lessons from greatest gurus, '*Your Leadership Playbook*' (Available at Amazon) reveals core techniques that is perfect answer to many tempting questions about results. What else? It provides you with infographics and workbook space to implement and make your own success blueprint. A small concise to-the-point book for action-takers.

BONUS #3: 1 Fee Waiver to 1-on-1 with Author & Trainer

Bishal Kumar is a Spreadsheet Lover, Author and has decade of experience working with World's Best MNCs and incubated multiple Startups. He is also known as consultant and external faculty in Engineering colleges. He will love to discuss any topic that can help you - Career Counseling, Interview, Google Sheets, Startup Mentor, Authorship, Pitch Presentation, or maybe a mix.

BONUS #4: Access to Private Facebook 'GSM' Community

A Private Facebook group with Google Sheets Lovers where Bishal will be personally active and helping to close any doubts and promote a learning environment.

Please do reach to 4pmtownhall.team@gmail.com/tobishalkumar@gmail.com for any queries, suggestions or opportunities; Bishal and Team will be more than happy to connect.

Another Book from Author Desk

'Your Leadership Playbook' available at Amazon and Notion Press.

There are only two things that can take you to a greatness of life - having dream and secondly self-motivation to keep you aligned with dream. The fact where most ends up is not having a right mentor, or a right push, or both.

Narrating 12 greatest mantras from his personal journey of leading teams and lessons from greatest gurus, this book reveals core techniques that is perfect answer to many questions. What else, it provides you with infographics and workbook space to implement and make your own success blueprint.